I0079972

BIBLICAL DISCIPLESHIP

THE PATH FOR HELPING

PEOPLE FOLLOW JESUS

DANIEL GOEPFRICH

Exegetica Publishing

2020

When asked "what is discipleship?" most people respond by saying it is being devoted to evangelism but little else. Some get technical and say, being a disciple means, "being a follower of Jesus." Daniel Goepfrich explains in *Biblical Discipleship* that discipleship has a learning curve which he systematically lays out. Goepfrich takes the Christian life from beginning to end, defining what salvation is and what it is not. After identifying many aspects of salvation (justification, redemption, imputation, adoption and more), he defines a path from spiritual infancy to childhood to adolescence and finally to adulthood – what is involved in being a disciple. *Biblical Discipleship* recognizes the importance of the Christian's rewards, warnings, and judgments and how they all factor into God's glory. To conclude, a sequence of eschatological events illustrates the Biblical view of things to come – for the believer and the unbeliever. This book is well worth considering for personal study or small group.

Robert Dick,
Director, Tyndale Learning Center,
New Hope Baptist Church, Parrish, FL

While salvation occurs in that brief moment when someone first believes in Christ for eternal life, discipleship is a lifelong process. Daniel Goepfrich's *Biblical Discipleship* is a breath of fresh air in a world that misconstrues these two vital doctrines. Not only does *Biblical Discipleship* set the record straight on the issue of salvation by grace, but it also lays out the course for a discipleship lifestyle that is Biblically derived with a dispensational perspective of things to come. Discipleship is the responsibility of all Christians, so Goepfrich presents this material in an accessible format with study questions for small groups or personal reflection. This is a great resource for explaining what believers should be doing with our lives as we await our glorious future.

Dr. Paul Miles,
Executive Director,
Grace Abroad Ministries, Lviv, Ukraine

Finally, someone gives discipleship a fair look in context of Biblical treatment. Daniel's strength is backed with his gift as a sound student and teacher of the word of God. He gives keen attention on salvation in the first three chapters and clearly expounds on what salvation is, what it includes, and what salvation is not. Biblical Discipleship is a gift and a tool for any small group, church setting, or Bible school student.

Rev. Peter Wabuti Odanga,
Diani Beach Fellowship,
Kenya, East Africa

Discipleship can be difficult to articulate, but Goepfrich makes it easy to understand. What is discipleship? When does it start? Does it ever end? What is the point of all of this? Most of these questions are explained in detail with logical illustrations. This book will get you started on a process he has called "the path" – a set of Biblical steps leading to maturity.

David Tubirye,
Field Coordinator,
Word of Life Fellowship, Rwanda

Discipleship is an enduring theme in the Bible, and each generation needs to discover afresh the what and how of it. Each generation also needs to discover it in the light of what the Bible says. I say this because practically all non-Christian religions and movements emphasize one kind of discipleship or other, and these ideas have such wide influence that Christians often look at this topic from the non-Christian perspective that they have received. This kind of evaluation does produce a certain kind of discipleship, but it is *not* Christian in nature. Discipleship is Christian in nature only if it is derived *Sola Scriptura*, uncontaminated by non-Christian philosophies. In this book the author introduces the *what* of the subject purely on the basis of the Bible. Once he does that, he explains the rest in a Biblical manner.

Discipleship has implications for every aspect of the Christian life. Every Christian needs to be a disciple of the right kind because it will affect not only our present but also our future. I highly endorse this book because it has been written on the basis of what the Bible says about discipleship.

Dr. Johnson C. Philip, PhD, ThD, DSc,
President,
Trinity Graduate School of Apologetics and Theology

Biblical Discipleship was clearly written by a man who has been teaching on the topic of Biblical discipleship for many years. From the outline of the book to the thought-provoking questions at the end of each chapter, this work reads very well, addressing pastors, teachers, and laymen alike – or in short, every believer. The author's passionate appeal to the reader is felt in every chapter and makes this book a surprising page-turner. *Biblical Discipleship* reflects deep Biblical insight into the topic at hand.

In 2 Timothy 3:16-17, God presents a clear goal for His people: They are meant to be *complete, thoroughly equipped for every good work.* The believers' spiritual maturity is expressed in their practical abilities to fulfill all that God has called them to do. The means by which this maturing is to be accomplished is by *all Scripture.* Often, God's goals turn into the believers' tasks. *We* are to make disciples. *We* are to teach our brothers and sisters in the Lord all Scripture so that they may be equipped for every good work.

Unfortunately, there is a profound lack of understanding in the churches today of what solid discipleship training entails. Often, even deacons and elders have a difficult time explaining what a Biblical disciple really is. The mark of a disciple is obedience, and a lifelong learner willing to sit at the feet of the Savior to study the Scriptures, to know Him better, to follow Him, and to serve Him. Daniel Goepfrich offers an easy to follow roadmap that allows every believer to fulfill God's calling to make disciples (Matthew 28:19-20). I highly recommend this book.

Christiane Jurik,
Director of Publications and Editor-in-Chief,
Ariel Ministries, San Antonio, TX

Daniel Goepfrich does a masterful job of explaining key components in a Biblical model for discipleship. The author sets a proper foundation for understanding the process of discipleship by distinguishing the Biblical doctrine of salvation from the spiritual life and growth of the believer in Christ which follows salvation. He also demonstrates that the ongoing process of discipleship has benefits to the believer in this life and in the life to come. Goepfrich sets forth eight steps along *the path* toward spiritual maturity in his exegesis of 2 Peter 1:5-7. These spiritual markers act as guideposts pointing the believer toward maturity in Christ and the goal of Christlikeness. It is in "The Spiritual Maturity Clock" wherein the author described the process of discipleship as four stages that the believer typically passes through on the path to maturity: "infant, child, young person, parent." Goepfrich explains that "...it is possible for us to identify where we are in our spiritual growth and discover and take the steps necessary to move to the next stage in our spiritual development. The more mature we become the more we will be able to help others grow as well, fulfilling the Great Commission of not just *being* disciples but *making* disciples."

Biblical Discipleship is a practical and common-sense tool for discipleship in the local church as well as in academic settings.

Dr. Don Trest,
Fellowship Bible Church,
Pass Christian, MS

Dr. Billy Graham once stated, "Salvation is free, but discipleship costs everything we have." In this book I have found one of the most complete, careful, and constructive manuals on the entire process of the gospel that I have seen in years. Dr. Goepfrich traces the gospel from the work of Christ, to faith alone in the Lord Jesus for redemption from sin, and the path of discipleship. His twenty years of research in this field has provided a manuscript worth its weight in gold. He even offers excellent comparisons to how the gospel of Christianity differs from cults and false world religions. Additionally, he touches on character traits of what mature godly disciples will exhibit. Traits like brotherly affection and unselfish love help this work retain a deep level of practicality that sadly some miss from too much time in the musty monastery-like academy circles.

One of my favorite sections of his work covers something not often seen from scholars or theologians from the American academy, a family motif or model of analysis of discipleship maturity. Familial theology permeates Scripture from Genesis to Revelation, yet the idea remains neglected in more circles than I care to think about. Yet in this manual the idea of maturity is rooted directly in the ideas that   the Apostle John taught us, with three or four ranks of maturity in disciples. John explained this concept by noting these levels of gospel maturity in familial terms: (1) little children (which would also include the infant category that Dr. Goepfrich highlighted), (2) young men and/or women, and (3) fathers and/or mothers in the faith, i.e. those who can reproduce others (see 1 John 2:12-14). Every evangelist, pastor, teacher, and elder would do well to have this book in their repertoire of armor to fulfill the Lord's command to make disciples (Matthew 28:18-20). I highly recommend the book, of course, but more importantly the theologian standing behind it, who exhibits both surgeon-like theological skill while having excellent theological bedside manner, an all too often rare combination.

Dr. Keith A. Sherlin, PhD, ThD, PhD(c),
Professor/Theologian/Author, Founder & Teacher
@ Christicommunity

Biblical Discipleship: The Path for Helping People Follow Jesus

By Daniel Goepfrich
www.theologyisforeveryone.com

Edited by Catherine Cone and Christiana Cone

© 2020 Daniel Goepfrich

ISBN – 978-0-9982805-5-4

www.exegeticapublishing.com
All rights reserved.

Unless otherwise indicated Scripture quotations are from The ESV® Bible (The Holy Bible, English Standard Version®), copyright © 2001 by Crossway, a publishing ministry of Good News Publishers. Used by permission. All rights reserved.
Quotations designated (NET) are from the NET Bible® copyright ©1996–2016 by Biblical Studies Press, L.L.C. All rights reserved.

"The Path" concept, name, outline, and all related subject material are used by permission from Oak Tree Community Church, South Bend, Indiana, USA. All rights reserved.

ACKNOWLEDGMENTS

There were several people who reviewed various drafts of this project. They helped find typographical errors, places where my thoughts and written words did not always connect, and sections that could be clarified.

Joleen Nakhla and Saralynn Goepfrich did all that and more. Their careful reading and critical questioning made this a far better work than it would have been without them. No one can tell how many times they read and reread each working draft, making comments along the way.

I want to thank Ben Noell and Gary Day for their patience and wisdom. Their insights and challenges to my assumptions and the doctrine presented here have been invaluable, especially for the section on discipleship. Specifically, Ben helped me think through and craft the overall section, focusing on what an ideal disciple looks like (see chapter eight: "The Characteristics of a Biblical Disciple"). Gary was the first to point out *the path*, and we spent countless hours studying and discussing how best to explain it in various ways (see chapter six: "Some Helpful Illustrations").

I also want to thank the members of Oak Tree Community Church in South Bend, Indiana, who have willingly listened and helped suggest analogies as I developed these teachings through various forms. For nearly two decades they have been subject to the doctrines presented here, embracing and working to practice and share them.

TABLE OF CONTENTS

INTRODUCTION

The church is in a state of crisis. In the United States, membership is declining across most denominations. Pastors and church leaders are falling in public scandals. Biblical doctrine is being replaced by feelings, experiences, and culture-driven ideology. Across the world, the church has been marginalized by apathy within and attacks from outside, or it has begun to assimilate ancient pagan practices that have stripped it of the powerful, life-changing impact it could have.

The solution for this is a return to *Biblical discipleship*. While the term *discipleship* is used frequently and discipleship programs are created and offered by church consultants and parachurch organizations, many churches and church leaders cannot say whether they are successfully making disciples or even what criteria they would use to determine that. The reason for this is due to at least four misunderstandings: 1) misunderstanding of what a Biblical disciple is, 2) misunderstanding the Biblical process for discipleship, 3) misunderstanding the difference between the singular Biblical process of discipleship and the multiplicity of methods and programs offered in place of a clear process, and 4) misunderstanding what salvation is and what it entails.

Sadly, for all the programs and curriculum that are offered, there is little written on what discipleship is and why it is important in this life and the life to come. This work is the result of nearly twenty years of research, study, reading, writing, and teaching on the topic of Biblical discipleship. This started in the church where I was born and grew up, both physically and in Christ, but since then I have been privileged to teach these principles to fellow believers in several other churches in the United States and other countries. Because making disciples—encouraging and building up one another to maturity in Christ—is the responsibility of every believer (Ephesians 4:11-16; Colossians 3:16), this book is written for all Christians, not just pastors or academics. It is my prayer that we all become actively involved in the Biblical process coming to know Jesus better and love him more and help others to do the same.

PART ONE
SALVATION

CHAPTER ONE

WHAT IS SALVATION?

Anyone who has spent time in church or around church people has likely heard either "believe in Jesus" or "put your faith in Jesus." But what does that mean? Believe what? Most people believe that he was real, even that he did great things. Islam teaches that Jesus was one of their greatest prophets. Nearly every major religion agrees that he was a good teacher and possibly even a miracle-worker. Does that mean that they "believe in Jesus"?

Can we believe just anything? What is the minimum that someone must believe, and how much does he or she have to *really* believe it? Are we allowed to not always be sure, to have questions, to sometimes wonder if it's true? Do we have to be completely certain all the time, no questions asked? Do we have to know and understand everything in the Bible to have faith?

These are all valid questions and concerns I have heard and addressed with people for many years because knowing these answers is key to everything else in Biblical Christianity.

The truth is that no one—again, no one at all—has complete faith or belief as described in some of those questions. No one has a complete understanding of the entire Bible to the point that they run out of questions to ask. Even the most faithful believers, pastors, and teachers are on a life-long journey of knowing Jesus better and loving him more. There is nothing wrong with having questions and wrestling with hard truths, but how much is necessary for salvation?

Fortunately for all of us, it is not necessary to know everything. However, the other extreme—that we can simply believe anything we want or nothing at all—is not true either. There are specific truths that our faith or belief must contain. About thirty years after Jesus' life, ministry, death, and resurrection, one of his closest friends and the apostles' chief spokesman, Peter, sent a letter to a specific group of people. Look how he addressed them: "To those who have obtained like precious faith with us by the righteousness of our God and Savior Jesus Christ" (2 Peter 1:1, NKJV).

'Like precious faith"– It seems that Peter had something very specific in mind that his readers believed and had in common with himself and the other apostles. However, since he did not define it in this letter, we must look to see if he did so somewhere else. He did.

In a sermon he preached years earlier, Peter insisted, "There is salvation in no one else, for there is no other name under heaven given among men by which we must be saved" (Acts 4:12). Not surprisingly, this is exactly what Jesus himself claimed: "I am the way, and the truth, and the life. No one comes to the Father except through me" (John 14:6). Paul made a similar statement to his young protégé: "For there is one God, and there is one mediator between God and men, the man Christ Jesus" (1 Timothy 2:5).

While that certainly sounds like good news[1], it introduces other questions: Why do we need to be saved in the first place? Why would we need someone to mediate between us and God? Can we not simply approach God ourselves? Aren't we all God's children as so many people say?

THE PROBLEM

It will come as no surprise to discover that the Bible says that humanity has a real problem. In fact, this is one of those areas where most world religions would agree—people are not perfect. Just read the headlines of any news site, and you cannot escape the violence, hatred, and, sometimes, just plain stupidity of others of our race.

Some might call these wrongs or imperfections or flaws or mistakes. The United States judicial system uses words like misdemeanor and felony for some of the bigger flaws. Many religions, though, use a different word, one found in the Bible: *sin.*

Sin is an interesting word because it does not sound anything like its basic meaning. The word may leave the impression of something dirty or forbidden: for example, "That dessert was sinfully delicious!" Now, while it can be applied that

---

[1] The word "gospel" comes from the Old English word *godspel* which meant "good story." The Greek word *euangelion* (εὐαγγέλιον) is where we get "evangelism" which also means "good news, story, message." The gospel is the good news about how we can be made right with God through Jesus.

way, that is not what it means. In the original language of the New Testament (first century common Greek), the word most often translated *sin* simply means to miss the mark.[2] This could be involuntary or intentional, but it is still a miss.

Think of almost any sport, and you will quickly find a correlation. Whether you are shooting a basketball, kicking a soccer ball, throwing a football, or firing an arrow or bullet, you have a goal or destination in mind for that object; you are aiming at a mark. To sin simply means that you missed. You aimed and missed. You might have been close, but close doesn't count.

So, what mark are we missing, what target have we been unable to hit? "All have sinned and fall short of the glory of God" (Romans 3:23). The target we should be shooting for is God's glory—the perfect, untarnished reputation of God and his character. At the very beginning of the Bible we find that "God created humankind in his own image" (Genesis 1:27, NET). Humanity was created and designed by God to accurately reflect everything God is. Look around and see; how are we doing? We have failed miserably! No one with an accurate concept of God could say that humanity has upheld our end of the deal. We have fallen short of God's glory. We have missed the mark. We have sinned.

So, What is the Problem?

Let's be honest—that doesn't sound like a big deal. So, we messed up. After all, we're not perfect, right? God cannot expect

---

[2] The Greek word is *hamartia* (ἁμαρτία). The theological term for the doctrine of sin is *hamartiology*.

us to hit the mark all the time, can he? Well, actually, yes, he can.

Consider this: if you invented something, would you not expect it to perfectly fulfill whatever you designed it to do? In fact, if your product failed to live up to its specifications, you would be disappointed. You would want to go back to the drawing board, review every minute detail to discover what went wrong, then make any corrections that you found, right? Of course, you would. You would not release that product to the public because your name and reputation are on the line. Maybe you have other products you want to sell. One bad design could ruin everything, especially if it harmed the people using it! The only option would be to fix it or throw it away.

Now consider this: the perfect God of the universe, who cannot make any mistakes or design flaws, created humanity using himself—his own character—as the pattern. It was his image, his likeness, on the blueprint (Genesis 1:26-27). Not only that, but he created the prototype with his own hands (Genesis 2:7). The first human was not outsourced to a third-party development and distribution channel. God did the work himself, every step of the way. What could go wrong?

It is at this point that our product illustration shifts direction. When God created humanity, he gave us something that a manufacturer cannot give an inanimate product: free will, also called "the power of contrary choice."[3] In what some might call a design flaw, God built into the first humans the ability to

---

[3] "The power of contrary choice" refers to the ability to choose something contrary to what the designer intended.

choose to break away from him, to choose to disobey him, to choose to contradict him. To make us truly free (like himself[4]), he had to allow us to walk away.

So, what can God do when his *product* fails? He has the same options as every other manufacturer—he must either salvage it or throw it away. Here is how the Bible puts it: "The wages of sin is death, but the free gift of God is eternal life in Christ Jesus our Lord" (Romans 6:23).

Anyone with a job understands the concept of wages. It is the payment received for the job done. A person works a certain number of hours or sells a certain number of items or fulfills some contracted work, and they receive a paycheck. That paycheck is what the company owes because of the work the person provided for them. Whether it is a guaranteed hourly rate or a fixed salary or a commission, withholding the payment the person earned is a serious matter.

The Bible says that the wages of sin—the amount owed to those who have missed the mark of perfectly reflecting God's glory—is death. This can mean physical death (the separation of body and soul) or spiritual death (the separation of an individual from God). If a simple earthly product that does not work must be thrown out, how much more do humans, who do not live up to their design of being completely perfect like God, deserve to be thrown out as well?

---

[4] The concept of being created in God's image (Genesis 1:26) is far-reaching and beyond the scope of what we can cover here, but to pattern us after himself meant instilling in us a level of freedom that we obviously cannot handle apart from him.

The devil who had deceived them was thrown into the lake of fire and sulfur where the beast and the false prophet were, and they will be tormented day and night forever and ever. ... This is the second death, the lake of fire. And if anyone's name was not found written in the book of life, he was thrown into the lake of fire (Revelation 20:10, 14-15).

According to Jesus, the purpose of this lake of fire is to punish the devil and his angels eternally for their horrific rebellion against God (Matthew 25:41). However, the Bible is also clear that humans who choose to follow the same path of rebellion against God—not meeting his perfect design—will be sentenced to the same eternal fate because the wages of sin is death.

But Wait...!

"Wait!" You might say. "Is there nothing that can be done? If some products can be salvaged, isn't there hope for humanity as well? What if we promise to do better? Won't God give us any credit for the good things we do? Can't we be salvaged?"

Think about a championship basketball game. Only one point separates two teams in the final seconds. Every eye in the gymnasium is on the best shooter on the team that is trailing. If he can make the clutch shot, his team wins; if not, they lose. Now, if that player misses the shot, will he be invited to the champions' celebration? Of course not; he missed the shot, and his entire team lost the game. Even if they lost by only one point, they still lost; they missed the mark. The game is over, and there is no way to salvage it.

The same is true with humanity and God. Once the game is over—once we have taken our last breath—there are no more chances. Any deficit we have against God's perfect character is the final score. This is the reason some people work so hard to be good; they are trying to build up points before the game is over.

The problem is that they do not take into consideration just how perfect God's character is. Even one violation of his character—one lie, one disobedience, one act of rebellion—puts us way behind. We can either be completely perfect like God or not perfect at all; there is no middle ground. To use a banking analogy[5], we are completely bankrupt, so far in debt with no spiritual assets to claim, that we can never dig ourselves out. How could we even get back to zero? If the wage for even one sin is death (Romans 6:23), how could a person work that off? Even if we never again committed even one sin and did only good for the rest of our lives, we still have that one mark against us that deserves death.

Much like in sports, the only way to change the final score is to add points while the game is still going. But if we cannot do enough good to make up for even one violation of God's infinite perfection, how could we possibly make up for all the bad in our lives?

THE SOLUTION

Like a designer who can change his or her flawed product to make it work as intended, God instituted a plan to fix

---

[5] The Biblical writers loved analogies to explain their points, especially sports and banking.

humanity's problem and put us back on track to reflecting him properly. A product cannot fix itself, and neither can a human. Only God can correct the flaw that we introduced when we chose to reject him.

Remember, "the wages of sin is death" (Romans 6:23); this is what we deserve and the only thing God owes us. That means that anything else he does is a gift. Consider the second half of that same verse: "For the wages of sin is death, **but the free gift of God is eternal life in Christ Jesus our Lord.**"

"The free gift of God" – It is a mistake to think that God hates people or does not want to see us succeed. We are his creation, made to reflect him. Why would he want us to fail? Why would he want to condemn our entire race to the lake of fire forever? He doesn't, but since we cannot fix ourselves, God had to step in and do it.

This brings up two important points. First, whatever God requires is *guaranteed* to work. If he said, "Stand on your head for ten minutes, and I will accept that," that is his prerogative, and it would be enough. Second, whatever God requires is the *only* thing that will work. Think of this as God's terms and conditions. If he is the only one who can salvage us and fix our problem, then 1) we must trust that he knows what he is doing and 2) we must acknowledge that those are the only terms he will accept. We cannot come to him on our own terms; we must humbly accept his terms or continue to walk away from him toward the lake of fire.

So, what are God's terms to fix our sin problem and to salvage our lives so we do not spend eternity separated from him? In other words, *what is the only way God provided for you and me to get right with him?* Nearly two millennia ago, a broken man asked the apostle Paul that very question. Here was his answer:

> Then [the man] brought [Paul and Barnabas] out and said, "Sirs, what must I do to be saved?" And they said, **"Believe in the Lord Jesus, and you will be saved**, you and your household" (Acts 16:30-31).

This is the gospel, the good news that everyone needs to hear. God requires only one thing: *believe*. So, back to the question from the very first page of this chapter: what must a person believe? A few years after this incident in Acts 16, the apostle Paul wrote a letter in which he clarified what he meant by *believe in the Lord Jesus*:

> I delivered to you as of first importance what I also received: that **Christ died for our sins in accordance with the Scriptures,** that he was buried, that **he was raised on the third day in accordance with the Scriptures** (1 Corinthians 15:3-4).

According to Paul, there are two things a person must believe: who Jesus is and what Jesus did. To believe in Jesus as Lord or Christ is to embrace the truth that he is the one sent from God to rescue humanity, that he is the only one who can do it, and that he accomplished it through his death and resurrection – nothing more, nothing less. It means to appropriate for yourself, personally and individually, the gift that God offers to everyone.

Since the wages of sin is death, for God to forgive sin, someone must die. This is the reason standing on our head for ten minutes or being baptized or committing to a life of service in a poverty-stricken country, or *anything else,* is not enough. The wages of sin is *death;* someone had to die. Jesus lived a sinless life so that he had no sin of his own to pay for. In God's gracious plan, he chose to accept Jesus' death in our place. Jesus substituted himself for us; he received the wages of our sin. In another conversation, Paul used the word *repent.*

> The times of ignorance God overlooked, but **now he commands all people everywhere to repent**, because he has fixed a day on which he will judge the world in righteousness by a man whom he has appointed; and of this he has given assurance to all by raising him from the dead (Acts 17:30-31).

In the Bible, *repent* refers to a change of mind, often or usually accompanied by a change in action based on new understanding.[6] In order to believe the truth, we must honestly consider it—the truth about ourselves and our sin, about Jesus and his death and resurrection, about the only way God allows and invites us to become right with him. God wants us to change our beliefs based on these truths.

Believing in Jesus alone for salvation means that we have reconsidered our position; we have *repented*, rejecting what we used to believe about these things and embracing the truth for ourselves. We must accept that only God can rescue us from sin

---

[6] The Greek word in the New Testament is *metanoeō* (μετανοέω), which is a compound word comprised of the preposition *meta,* "after," and *noeō,* "to grasp, understand, comprehend." So, to repent means to understand something after something else occurs, i.e., a change of understanding.

and eternal judgment, and we submit ourselves to his terms and conditions. That is all that God requires for a person to begin a new relationship with him. Are you prepared to come to terms with the truth?

1. Every person is a sinner, separated from God.

   All have sinned and fall short of the glory of God (Romans 3:23).

2. Jesus died for all sinners, even when we were still sinners.

   God shows his love for us in that **while we were still sinners, Christ died for us** (Romans 5:8).

3. Our path to God goes only through Jesus.

   There is one God, and **there is one mediator between God and men, the man Christ Jesus**, who gave himself as a ransom for all, which is the testimony given at the proper time (1 Timothy 2:5-6).

4. There is nothing we can do except believe and accept the truth.

   By grace you have been saved through faith. And this is not your own doing; it is the gift of God, not a result of works, **so that no one may boast** (Ephesians 2:8-9).

5. Everyone who accepts God's gift in God's way is guaranteed eternal life.

   For God so loved the world, that he gave his only Son, that **whoever believes in him should not perish but have eternal life** (John 3:16).

Although only a new belief and acceptance of the truths given above is all that God requires to give a person his salvation, many people find it helpful to say a short prayer. It verbalizes what the person now believes and allows them to thank God for his gracious gift. It is also a great start to a new life of talking with God through prayer.

The words provided below are not magic. Saying them means nothing if your heart has not changed, but you might find them helpful as you talk to God from your heart.

God, thank you for showing me this truth about me and my sin. I do know that I have fallen short of your perfection and your design for me, and I accept that there is nothing I can do to fix it and make myself right with You. Thank you for sending Jesus to die in my place because of my sins and for beating death by bringing him back to life. Thank you for offering to forgive me completely when I come to you on your terms. I do believe; I do trust that this is the only way you allow. I do accept him as the only way to have a good relationship with you. Thank you for saving me. Thank you, Jesus, for dying for me. Help me to learn to understand this better so I can continue to grow in my gratitude and love toward you.

STUDY QUESTIONS

1. What is sin?

2. Why did Jesus have to die on the cross?

3. What is required for you to become right with God?

4. What is the danger in adding to or subtracting any of the truths explained in this chapter?

5. Do you believe the message given in this chapter? Could you confidently share it with someone else?

6. What is the most important truth, principle, or practice you learned from this chapter? What do you plan to do with it?

CHAPTER TWO

WHAT HAPPENS AT SALVATION?

Chapter one explained what salvation is, why we need it, and how we can receive it as a gift from God. Often, when people think of salvation, they imagine forgiveness of their sins and going to heaven. While those things are certainly true, as we look through the Bible, we find that there are many more events that take place in or for a person when he or she believes in Jesus. While we could say that these are the things that happen at salvation, it may be more accurate to say that all these things together make up what we call eternal salvation. Far more than just forgiveness and a right relationship with God, there are at least seventeen different events, transactions, and changes that take place when a person believes in Jesus as Savior.

Because most of these happen simultaneously, we cannot put them into chronological order. However, we can think of them in *logical* order because certain events are logically based on others. For instance, God cannot declare a person to be not guilty (justification) until after He has forgiven that person's sin (remission) and given that person Jesus' righteousness (imputation). So, logically speaking, remission and imputation must take place before justification, although, in reality, they happen immediately when a person believes.

In this chapter, we explore these events, explaining the terms, and providing Scriptural support for this amazing gift we underwhelmingly call salvation. While the (logical) order of some of these can be debated, the fact that they occur as part of salvation cannot.

REDEMPTION

God's first act when a person believes in Jesus is the process of redemption. To redeem something means that we trade or convert one thing, like a coupon or ticket, for something else. The value of the coupon—what it is worth—is usually stated clearly. This means that it cannot be traded for just anything, only for what it was intended.

In the New Testament, redemption is described as having three aspects based on three different words and word pictures.[7] This shows that redemption takes place in several stages, both before and at the moment of salvation.

Purchase

The first aspect of redemption is purchase. The Greek word is *agorazō* (ἀγοράζω) from which we get the word *Agora*—

---

[7] It is essential to remember that word pictures and analogies can go only so far to explain reality. They almost always break down at some point, and when they are used to illustrate something as great as eternal salvation, we should expect that they may not always give as full of a picture as we would like.

the marketplace.[8] It was the place where goods and services (including slaves) were publicly bought, sold, and traded. Even a quick glance through the Gospels and Acts show that many of Jesus' and the apostles' interactions and teachings occurred in public areas (walking down the street, in the public temple area, in the synagogues, in open fields, etc.).

The Bible describes the spiritual state of unbelievers as Satan's slaves. The popular concept that Satan collects souls is a myth. The Bible regularly calls and portrays him as one who seeks to destroy people, not collect them.[9] He has no interest in keeping people; he simply wants to make sure that we do not turn in faith to God.

On the other hand, the idea that Satan does have some control over people (holds them in slavery, Hebrews 2:14-15) shows that humans are not as free as we like to think we are. The apostles repeatedly wrote that, without Christ, we are slaves to Satan, sin, and death.[10] However, all slaves have a purchase price, and, in this illustration, the price to purchase us for himself was the death of Christ.

> You were **bought with a price**. So glorify God in your body (1 Corinthians 6:20).

> False prophets also arose among the people, just as there will be false teachers among you, who will secretly bring

---

[8] *Agoraphobia* is the fear of being in public places, like the marketplace.

[9] Consider what he did when God gave him free rein over Job (Job 1-2). In Hebrews he is described as having the power of death that he holds over people (Hebrews 2:14-15).

[10] See, for example, Romans 6:16; 2 Peter 2:19; 1 John 5:19.

in destructive heresies, even denying the Master **who bought them**, bringing upon themselves swift destruction (2 Peter 2:1).

Not for Resale

Sometimes owners would purchase slaves just to place them back on the market later for more money (much like investors buy and sell, or flip houses today). According to Scripture, God not only purchased our lives at the cross, but he also removed us from the slave market forever. This Greek word (*exagorazō*, ἐξαγοράζω) is similar to the first one, but it adds a prefix to the front (*ex-*) that means *out of.* God purchased us with Jesus' blood and took us out of the market. Once a person has been saved, God never makes them available for anyone else.

> Christ **redeemed** us from the curse of the law by becoming a curse for us—for it is written, Cursed is everyone who is hanged on a tree—so that in Christ Jesus the blessing of Abraham might come to the Gentiles, so that we might receive the promised Spirit through faith (Galatians 3:13-14).

Release

When slaves were purchased from the market, they were expected to serve at the master's pleasure. Whatever the master said was law for his slaves. This included not only the rules the master chose to enforce but the freedoms as well.

Contrary to popular Western understanding, many slave owners were not monsters. They did not beat and torture their slaves or treat them like dirt. The reason for this was not moral or ethical; it was often financial. A slave was more than a commodity; he was an investment. For every slave who died or ran away, the owner needed to purchase more, and this could get very expensive. It was much more profitable to treat his slaves well enough that they would not think it worth trying to escape, even if the work was hard.

Under the Mosaic Law that God set up for Israel, this went even further. People would often sell themselves into slavery to pay off debt. Once the debt was paid, they were released; the slavery had served its purpose. On occasion, a slave would find such a good master that God allowed the newly freed person to voluntarily bind himself to that master for the rest of his life. This position was called a bondservant or bondslave, and it required a ceremony and witnesses to make it official.[11] Once this option was chosen, there was no return.

There is much similarity between these ancient practices and the redemption that comes at salvation. When a person believes in Jesus as Savior, he or she is purchased and removed from the market—no longer a slave to Satan and sin. At this point, however, the Scriptures say that we are not immediately made slaves of our new owner (God). The third word for redemption is *lutroō* (λυτρόω)—to set free.

> He gave himself for us **to set us free** from every kind of lawlessness and to purify for himself a people who are truly his, who are eager to do good (Titus 2:14, NET).

Unlike those normally bought on the market, this purchase does not require us to serve God like slaves. Rather

---

[11] Exodus 21:5-6; Deuteronomy 15:16-17.

than forcing his lordship on us, God desires that we choose to submit ourselves to him. He wants us to voluntarily become his *bondservants*, not force us to be his *slaves*. After we believe, God desires us to bow to him as our Lord or Master as an act of willful gratitude for his love and grace and mercy on our behalf. This is rarely done immediately at salvation, although we are free to do so, and it certainly is not a prerequisite to obtaining salvation.[12] God has freed us to serve either him or ourselves, but he offers the best life (and eternal rewards[13]) only to those who choose to submit to serving him.

REMISSION

Remit and remission have several meanings: to send payment, to decrease (like a disease goes in remission), and to forgive or pardon. In this context, we mean to forgive or pardon. The Greek word, *aphēsis* (ἀφησις), occurs seventeen times in the New Testament and refers to release or freedom, almost every time due to the forgiveness from sin.[14]

In sermons, classes, and discussions about salvation, this is the aspect that we usually emphasize. When a person believes in Jesus as Savior, God forgives his or her sins forever. While this is a small piece of the overall puzzle, as noted at the beginning of this chapter, it is still an important piece. It is at

[12] See chapter three on what salvation is not for further explanation on this point.

[13] See chapter nine for more information about how believers will be rewarded.

[14] See Matthew 26:28; Mark 1:4; 3:29; Luke 1:77; 3:3; 24:47; Acts 2:38; 5:31; 10:43; 13:38; 26:18; Ephesians 1:7; Colossians 1:14; Hebrews 9:22; 10:18.

this point—immediately after we believe—that God must deal with our sin.

> And you were dead in the trespasses and sins... (Ephesians 2:1).

In the Bible, death always refers to a kind of separation. Physical death is when the soul separates from the body. Even people who do not believe Biblical doctrine often attend funerals, look at the body in the casket, and say things like, "They are in a better place." Somehow, we know that a separation has taken place, and the *real* person is no longer housed in the body in front of us.

The Scriptures also speak of spiritual death, the separation of an individual from God at the spiritual level. According to Paul, we come into this world "dead in [our] trespasses and sins...and were by nature children of wrath" (Ephesians 2:1-3). When we are physically born, we are spiritually dead, subject to God's wrath because of our sin. If we were to physically die while still in that spiritual state, we would be separated from God for eternity, what John called "the second death" (Revelation 20:6, 14).

Because "the wages of sin is death" (Romans 6:23), God must forgive our sin—pardon and release us from his wrath against sin—before he can do everything else that the salvation package includes. How can he do this? How are the wages of our sin paid? He does this based on Jesus' death.

> I delivered to you as of first importance what I also received: that **Christ died for our sins** in accordance with the Scriptures, that he was buried, that he was raised on

the third day in accordance with the Scriptures (1 Corinthians 15:3-4).

It is essential to remember that God does not offer his pardon/forgiveness based on his love or grace. Our sin violated his holiness, and his eternal justice demands payment. If he could forgive just because he wanted to do so, then we would find him to be capricious. If he can grant forgiveness arbitrarily, he can take it away without reason as well, and that should scare us. An erratic God, who can change his demands at any second, can offer no true hope or peace and certainly cannot guarantee anything for eternity.

If, however, God offers his pardon as the result of the payment made through Jesus' death, and if he offers that pardon to everyone equally, then he is right and just to grant it to everyone who accepts his terms and withhold it from everyone who rejects them. This is exactly the picture that we find throughout Scripture. In remission, our sin is completely removed from us, and God grants us a complete pardon.

As far as the east is from the west, **so far does he remove our transgressions from us** (Psalm 103:12).

In him we have redemption through his blood, **the forgiveness of our trespasses**, according to the riches of his grace... (Ephesians 1:7).

...in whom we have redemption, **the forgiveness of sins** (Colossians 1:14).

REGENERATION

The word regenerate comes from the Latin *regenerātus*, following the underlying Greek word, *palingenesia* (παλινγενεσια). The Greek *palin* and Latin *re* both mean again.[15] So what happens again? *Generātus* and *genesia*[16] both are forms of words that mean to bring forth, beget, give birth. The full Greek word occurs only twice in the New Testament, once when Jesus mentioned that the earth will be renewed in his kingdom (Matthew 19:28) and once when Paul described what the Holy Spirit does in a person at salvation.

> He saved us, not because of works done by us in righteousness, but according to his own mercy, **by the washing of regeneration** and renewal of the Holy Spirit (Titus 3:5).

A similar phrase is found in the well-known discussion between Jesus and Nicodemus in John 3. Most English Bibles translate Jesus' words as "You must be born again" (John 3:3).[17] Nothing else in the salvation process can happen until a person experiences this new birth.

---

[15] English still frequently uses *re-* as a prefix for *again*, for example, redo, retake, reapply, etc.

[16] This is where we get the name of the first book of the Bible—Genesis. It means the birth or beginning.

[17] John recorded two words (*gennēthē anōthen*, γεννηθη ἀνωθεν) which can mean either born again or born from above. It is most likely that Jesus meant from above, although Nicodemus clearly understood it as born again.

In the previous section on remission, we saw that when we are born physically, we are still dead spiritually. This is the reason that regeneration is necessary. In order to be saved or delivered from eternal spiritual death and punishment, we must be pardoned from God's wrath against our sin, then we must be born again. Immediately after God pardons us, he gives us a brand-new spiritual life.

Another word that John used to describe this experience was *metabainō* (μεταβαίνω)—to pass over. John quoted Jesus saying this once and then used it in his own teaching to describe a person's crossing from spiritual death into spiritual life.

> Truly, truly, I say to you, whoever hears my word and believes him who sent me has eternal life. He does not come into judgment **but has passed from death to life** (John 5:24).

> We know that **we have passed out of death into life**, because we love the brothers. Whoever does not love abides in death (1 John 3:14).

Summary #1

In these first three steps, for everyone who comes to him through Jesus, God purchased us out of the slave market, pardoned us from his eternal wrath against our sin, and gave us spiritual life.

IMPUTATION

The Bible describes the natural human state as completely, spiritually bankrupt before God. We are so far spiritually depraved,[18] that we cannot do enough good to even break even with God, yet, breaking even is all forgiveness (remission) can accomplish.

> The heart is deceitful above all things, and desperately sick; who can understand it (Jeremiah 17:9)?

If the salvation package stopped with the forgiveness of our sin and provided nothing further, we would essentially be like Adam and Eve at the beginning of Genesis—innocent but able to become guilty again. We would be back to zero, meaning we could easily fall back into the same spiritual mess we are in now. This is where imputation comes in.

Imputation comes from a Latin word that means to ascribe (which does not help most of us!). Practically speaking, it means to transfer or place something onto someone else. This

---

[18] Depravity is a favorite word for some theologians, and how they define it determines much of their beliefs about salvation. To be depraved means to be corrupted. Total depravity, then, means either 1) corruption to the point that a person is completely unable to do any good at all or 2) corruption that extends to every part of the person. The first definition logically concludes that a person does not even have the faith to respond to Jesus unless God gives it to them first. The second definition means that, while the person has been spiritually corrupted, they still have the image of God impressed upon them and are able to respond in faith when they hear the gospel in conjunction with the general convicting work of the Holy Spirit (John 16:8-11). Chapter three will deal with this in more detail.

could mean to charge them with a crime, to identify them as having a specific character trait, or to give them something.

Theologically, the Bible speaks of three imputations or transfers that take place with respect to salvation: Adam to people, people to Jesus, and Jesus to people.

Adam to People

The first transfer happened long before you and I were born. In Genesis 3:6, Adam deliberately broke the single law that God had placed on him—he ate the fruit God had forbidden. At that moment, Adam became a sinner, that is, his basic nature became inherently sinful, constantly leaning and leading him away from God. The obvious result of this is evident in the fact that his first action was to try to hide from God (Genesis 3:8-10). The relationship that humanity had with God was damaged. However, that is not the whole story. If Adam had a sinful nature, that would be bad, but something else occurred that Adam had not considered. Just like God had created the animals to reproduce after themselves, including all their traits and qualities, he created people to do the same thing.

> When Adam had lived 130 years, he fathered a son **in his own likeness, after his image**, and named him Seth (Genesis 5:3).

Before Adam had sinned, this would not have been a problem. He was created after God's image and likeness (Genesis 1:27) and would have reproduced the same. But after he sinned, he passed down his flawed, sinful nature. This is the first imputation; all humanity receives a sinful nature from

Adam passed down through their fathers.[19] Paul was very clear that sin came to humanity through one man.

> Just as **sin came into the world through one man**, and death through sin, and so death spread to all men because all sinned (Romans 5:12).

People to Jesus

The second imputation happened on the cross. Just like the guilt of Adam's sin was transferred to all humanity, God transferred the guilt of our sin to Jesus so that his death would serve as the payment, the wages of sin.

> God made the one who did not know sin **to be sin for us**.... (2 Corinthians 5:21a, NET).

> I delivered to you as of first importance what I also received: that **Christ died for our sins** in accordance with the Scriptures... (1 Corinthians 15:3).

Christ died *for* our sins. We should not take this to mean just that he died *because of* our sins. Paul's choice of words indicates substitution, not just purpose. While it is true that Jesus died because of our sins, it was much more than that. Jesus died for them, on behalf of them, in our place. By dying for our sins, Jesus

---

[19] It is debated whether the sinful nature comes from both father and mother (like biological DNA) or just the father. There are significant theological reasons to believe that only the father passes the sinful nature, not the least of which is the fact that Jesus was fully human (biologically through Mary) yet without a sinful nature. Others have different ways to explain how that happened, but it does not change the fact that our sinful nature originally came from Adam.

secured the payment so that we would not have to die for them ourselves. The only way that Jesus could pay for our sins was if that guilt was transferred to him. He was charged for our crime and served the sentence handed down by God himself. This satisfied God's wrath against our sins.

> My little children, I am writing these things to you so that you may not sin. But if anyone does sin, we have an advocate with the Father, Jesus Christ the righteous One, and **he himself is the atoning sacrifice for our sins**, and not only for our sins but also for the whole world (1 John 2:1-2, NET).

Jesus to people

There is one more transfer that the Bible says takes place. Again, if everything stopped here—Adam's sin to us then our sin onto Jesus—we could be innocent again, but we could also become sinful again. What would keep us from simply going back to our corrupt ways?

Although Jesus died to pay for everyone's sin, not everyone will accept that. Many people refused to believe in Jesus; instead, they try to be good enough, hoping that their own goodness can overshadow their inherent sinfulness. Because of Jesus' death, those attempts are both unnecessary and unproductive. In the third imputation, all of Jesus' perfect righteousness is transferred to a person when he or she comes to Jesus in faith for salvation. In an eternally unfair trade, Jesus took our sin and exchanged it for his righteousness. Essentially, at salvation, our bank account with God goes from infinitely negative, with no hope of paying it off, to infinitely positive, with no chance of ever going back into debt. Forever, every believer has a new status with God. As he looks on us, he no longer sees our sin but Jesus' sinlessness. Here is the rest of a verse we only partially quoted above:

> God made the one who did not know sin to be sin for us, **so that in him we would become the righteousness of God** (2 Corinthians 5:21, NET).

The righteousness we have is not our own. It is part of the gift of God, credited to our personal accounts the moment we believed in Jesus.

> ...and be found in him, **not having a righteousness of my own that comes from the law, but that which comes through faith in Christ**, the righteousness from God that depends on faith (Philippians 3:9).

JUSTIFICATION

Just as remission and imputation are banking terms, justification is a legal term that refers to the official ruling God makes about a person. To be justified means that someone is officially declared not guilty.[20]

Imagine standing before God's court. You are the defendant; God is the judge. Before salvation, you are guilty of sin, because of both your sinful nature and your sinful actions. As you stand there awaiting his verdict, there is no question. The only thing he could say is, "Guilty!"

---

[20] If someone claims that you are trying to justify a bad decision, they mean that you are trying to declare that your bad decision was, in reality, good.

You were dead in the trespasses and sins in which you once walked, following the course of this world, following the prince of the power of the air, the spirit that is now at work in the sons of disobedience—among whom we all once lived in the passions of our flesh, carrying out the desires of the body and the mind, **and were by nature children of wrath,** like the rest of mankind (Ephesians 2:1-3).

Once a person has had his or her bankruptcy pardoned (remission) and Jesus' righteousness credited (imputation), the only legitimate verdict God can make without violating his righteous character is "Not guilty!" God cannot look at a person with Jesus' righteousness, determine that he or she is still guilty, and be a just God. To condemn a person after God has removed his guilt and replaced it with righteousness would make him an unjust God, and his offer of salvation would be meaningless. However, by declaring his verdict after these other legal actions, God remains perfectly just when he declares a person not guilty.[21]

God publicly displayed him at his death as the mercy seat accessible through faith. This was to demonstrate his righteousness, because God in his forbearance had passed over the sins previously committed. This was also to demonstrate his righteousness in the present time, **so**

---

[21] As we will see, this does not mean that we no longer sin. Justification refers to our eternal status before God, not our day-to-day fellowship with him.

that he would be just and the justifier of the one who lives because of Jesus' faithfulness (Romans 3:25-26, NET).

There is therefore now **no condemnation for those who are in Christ Jesus** (Romans 8:1).

RECONCILIATION

We usually define reconciliation as bringing into agreement or harmony. Because of sin, nothing in creation is in harmony with God as he intended. One day, however, everything in all creation will be reconciled to God. Paul defines this as when everyone will finally agree with God about who Jesus truly is. This acknowledgment will be based on the fact of his death and resurrection.

> Therefore God has highly exalted him and bestowed on him the name that is above every name, so that at the name of Jesus **every knee should bow, in heaven and on earth and under the earth, and every tongue confess that Jesus Christ is Lord**, to the glory of God the Father (Philippians 2:9-11).

> For in him all the fullness of God was pleased to dwell, and through him **to reconcile to himself all things**, whether on earth or in heaven, **making peace by the blood of his cross** (Colossians 1:19-20).

This has obviously not happened yet, so we must believe it is still a future event. At salvation, however, believers do come into a special reconciliation with God right away through Jesus and his death. Once God has legally declared us to be righteous (justification), we are no longer enemies against him but have come into a new harmonious relationship with him. This is not a forced bowing of heads and knees before him, but rather our humble, willful decision to recognize him as the Savior, the only one sent by God who can bring us into a right relationship with him. In fact, this is exactly the message we are to share with this world, that they should come to him now, too, while they still have the choice.

> For **if while we were enemies we were reconciled to God by the death of his Son**, much more, now that we are reconciled, shall we be saved by his life (Romans 5:10).

> All this is from God, **who through Christ reconciled us to himself** and gave us the ministry of reconciliation; that is, in Christ God was reconciling the world to himself, not counting their trespasses against them, **and entrusting to us the message of reconciliation** (2 Corinthians 5:18-19).

Summary #2

In these next three steps, through Jesus' death on the cross, God transferred Jesus' righteousness to every believer, meaning that he can declare us not guilty, which brings us into a new relationship with him as friends instead of enemies.

THE HOLY SPIRIT

One of the greatest gifts a believer has is God's Holy Spirit living inside of us. He plays numerous roles, all of which are integral to our eternal salvation and our spiritual growth in this life. In this section, we will explore the five important works that take place or begin when a person believes and is saved.

Indwelling

Immediately when we believe in Jesus, the Holy Spirit spiritually takes up residence in us. Before this, he worked to convict us of our sin and bring us to faith in Jesus (John 16:8), but now he moves in and starts to work from the inside.

> Do you not know that you are God's temple and that **God's Spirit dwells in you?** (1 Corinthians 3:16).

Because of the close connection between the Father, Son, and Spirit, sometimes the Holy Spirit is called the Spirit of Christ, and Paul said that the Spirit's presence is effectively the same as having Christ himself in us.

> I have been crucified with Christ. It is no longer I who live, but **Christ who lives in me.** And the life I now live in the flesh I live by faith in the Son of God, who loved me and gave himself for me (Galatians 2:20).

This presence of the Holy Spirit is exceptionally important because a person without the Spirit is not saved at all.

> You, however, are not in the flesh but in the Spirit, if in fact the Spirit of God dwells in you. **Anyone who does not have the Spirit of Christ does not belong to him** (Romans 8:9).

This leads us to at least two conclusions. First, the Spirit must indwell a person immediately when he or she believes, or faith is not enough for salvation; something else must be necessary.

Second, the Spirit's presence must be permanent in each believer, otherwise, salvation could be lost. A theology which teaches that salvation can be lost has to explain how God could change his verdict from not guilty to guilty and how Jesus' imputed righteousness is not enough. Once a person believes and God begins opening the salvation package, there is nothing that can reverse it. Real salvation (as offered in the Bible) is *eternal* salvation. This is solidified by the Spirit's next action in the new believer.

Sealing

Upon indwelling a new believer, one of the Spirit's first actions is to seal him or her. In ancient times, like today, a seal on a box or crate could achieve several things: identification (what is inside), ownership (to whom it belongs), and security ("Do not use if this seal is broken"). In the same way, the Holy Spirit inside a believer acts as a type of seal on that person.

Notice in the following passages that the Holy Spirit accomplishes all three of these in his role as our seal. First, he identifies us as believers in Christ. Only those who are saved have the Holy Spirit, and everyone who has the Spirit is saved.

> In him you also, when you heard the word of truth, the gospel of your salvation, and believed in him, **were sealed with the promised Holy Spirit**, who is the guarantee of our inheritance until we acquire possession of it, to the praise of his glory (Ephesians 1:13-14).

> Anyone who does not have the Spirit of Christ **does not belong to him** (Romans 8:9b).

Second, the Spirit reveals our new ownership and keeps us only for God. Since God redeemed us, we now belong to him; we are his own possession. The redemption Paul referenced in Ephesians 1:14 is not when God bought us through Jesus' death but when he finally gets to take physical possession. This will happen when Jesus comes to take us to be with him (1 Thessalonians 4:13-18).[22]

Third, the Spirit as our seal achieves security. This speaks to whether a person's salvation can be lost or taken away for any reason. By placing His Holy Spirit inside us as a seal, God has guaranteed safe delivery, ensuring that no believer could ever be lost. The Spirit will perfectly seal and protect every believer until that day of physical redemption.

> Do not grieve the Holy Spirit of God, by whom **you were sealed for the day of redemption** (Ephesians 4:30).

> This is the will of him who sent me, that **I should lose nothing of all that he has given me** but raise it up on the last day (John 6:39).

Although not mentioned above, there is a fourth benefit we receive from the Holy Spirit as our seal. By identifying and securing us as God's possession, God considers the Holy Spirit to be a down payment of many more blessings to come. As if his

---

[22] This concept should not be surprising or confusing. There are many times that we may purchase something but not take possession immediately (like waiting for a purchase to be delivered). In the same way, although God has purchased us, we are still here on earth and will not physically be present with him until later.

own Spirit indwelling and sealing us were not enough, God said that is just a taste of what is to come. What an amazing gift!

> It is God who establishes us with you in Christ, and has anointed us, and who has also put his seal on us and **given us his Spirit in our hearts as a guarantee** (2 Corinthians 1:21-22).

Spirit Baptism

One of the most misunderstood works of the Holy Spirit is Spirit baptism. Depending on your church background, you may have been taught that this is something that you had to pray, beg, or fast to receive at some point after you believed. You may think it should come with a variety of supernatural signs (speaking in tongues, uncontrollable spasms, etc.) On the other hand, you may know next to nothing about Spirit baptism. Your church may have minimized it to the point that it was effectively non-existent in your belief system. Sadly, both of those extremes are dangerous and unbiblical. The baptism of the Spirit is a wonderful gift that is important to understand.

The Greek verb for baptism is *baptizo* (βαπτίζω), which simply means to immerse. It does not specify what is being immersed or immersion into what. It can be as simple as washing a cup or plate under water or dipping a piece of bread in oil. The obvious example is water baptism during which a person is fully immersed in water.[23]

---

[23] While it is true that not all churches practice full immersion, other forms (pouring, sprinkling, splashing, etc.) do not accurately represent the actual meaning of the term or its theological significance. It is worth noting that the water baptisms described in the Bible show the people

Because the same word is used for Spirit baptism, with nothing to indicate that the meaning has changed, we must interpret Spirit baptism to be the Spirit's immersion of someone into something. This is exactly how Paul describes and defines it.

> For **in one Spirit we were all baptized into one body**— Jews or Greeks, slaves or free—and all were made to drink of one Spirit (1 Corinthians 12:13).

Reviewing the context of 1 Corinthians 12, we discover that the "one body" is the "body of Christ", which Paul elsewhere says is the church.

> He put all things under his feet and gave him as head over all things to **the church, which is his body**, the fullness of him who fills all in all (Ephesians 1:22-23).

> **He is the head of the body, the church.** He is the beginning, the firstborn from the dead, that in everything he might be preeminent (Colossians 1:18).

> For as in one body we have many members, and the members do not all have the same function, **so we, though many, are one body in Christ**, and individually members one of another (Romans 12:4-5).

When a person believes in Jesus for salvation and the Holy Spirit comes into that person to indwell him or her, he immediately immerses or places the new believer into the body

---

going down into and coming back up out of a body of water (see Matthew 3:16; Acts 8:38-39).

of Christ, the church. This creates an unbreakable union between the new believer and Jesus himself.

There is another important point about this immersion. While the Greek word does indicate immersion *into* something, it never speaks to the removal of the thing immersed. In other words, baptism is a one-way action. Now, when it comes to water baptism, it is important that we bring the person back up out of the water (for obvious reasons)! However, technically, bringing them back out is not part of the baptism; that was done when they were submerged.

Why is this significant? Once the Holy Spirit immerses or places a believer into the body of Christ, the baptism is over. Nowhere in Scripture does it indicate that we ever come back out of the body or that this special connection with Jesus is ever broken. In fact, the other functions (like the seal), indicate the opposite; once we are in, we cannot come out, fall out, or be kicked out.

Unlike Spirit baptism, emerging from the water makes water baptism a great visual illustration of our identification with Jesus' death and resurrection. In the same way that Jesus died once (going into the water), was buried once (held under the water), and was resurrected once (coming back out of the water), so the Spirit baptizes us into his body just once, and we live looking forward to our resurrection.[24]

---

[24] It is worth noting that nearly every mention of baptism in the New Testament refers to Spirit baptism, not water baptism. In fact, when water baptism is meant, it is always clearly identified as such. When baptism is mentioned without any clarification, we should understand it

Do you not know that all of us **who have been baptized into Christ Jesus** were baptized into his death? We were buried therefore with him by baptism into death, in order that, just as Christ was raised from the dead by the glory of the Father, we too might walk in newness of life. For if we have been united with him in a death like his, we shall certainly be united with him in a resurrection like his (Romans 6:3-5).

Spiritual Gifts

After uniting us with Jesus and his church in Spirit baptism, the Holy Spirit distributes *spiritual gifts* to empower us to fulfill Jesus' command to love one another and help each other grow (make disciples). A spiritual gift is the supernatural outworking of the Holy Spirit so that one Christian ministers to fellow Christians. Every Christian is empowered in at least one way and is responsible for submitting to the Holy Spirit to use his gifts to help other believers grow.

Now there are varieties of gifts, but the same Spirit; and there are varieties of service, but the same Lord; and there are varieties of activities, but it is the same God who empowers them all in everyone. **To each is given the manifestation of the Spirit for the common good.** ... All these are empowered by one and the same Spirit, who apportions to each one individually as he wills (1 Corinthians 12:4-7, 11).

---

to mean Spirit baptism. This helps clear up several passages that people often find confusing (for example, Mark 16:16; 1 Peter 3:21).

The Bible speaks of these gifts and lists them in 1 Corinthians 12:8-10, 28-30; Romans 12:5-8; Ephesians 4:11; and 1 Peter 4:10-11. While many people have written and taught about spiritual gifts and different organizations offer assessments to help people identify their gifts, probably the most important step a believer can take is just to get involved serving somewhere. Often, that is the best way to determine how God has equipped us to serve most effectively. On the other hand, knowing one's gift without using it is pointless and unfruitful.

Illumination

The Scriptures assert that an unsaved person cannot understand spiritual truths. This does not mean they cannot understand the words on the pages of the Bible because God designed the Scriptures so that anyone can read and understand them. However, it is impossible to grasp the spiritual truths and principles that the Bible teaches without the Holy Spirit's help. This is the reason it is futile to try to reason with an unbeliever or answer all their questions before they will believe. We cannot *reason* or *argue* someone to faith in Jesus. However, at salvation, when the Holy Spirit indwells a new believer, that person receives a great new ability to understand and apply spiritual truth. Another word people use instead of illumination is enlightenment, but that word has been usurped by eastern mystics and their religions, so it may be best to not use it lest we confuse someone.

Of course, our new ability to understand does not mean that we will understand everything automatically. It still takes a great deal of time and effort to come to know the Scriptures well and to know God, but it is the Holy Spirit who makes this possible. No Christian has an excuse for not reading, studying, and understanding God's Word.

> As it is written, "What no eye has seen, nor ear heard, nor the heart of man imagined, what God has prepared for those who love him"—**these things God has revealed to us through the Spirit**. For the Spirit searches everything, even the depths of God. … Now we have received not the spirit of the world, but the Spirit who is from God, **that we might understand the things freely given us by God** (1 Corinthians 2:9-10, 12).

ADOPTION

In human families, adoption is the process by which a person, usually a child, is transferred from one family (or someone without a family) into a new family through a legally-binding action. Once the adoption is completed, the child has new parents and sometimes even a new name. This is one aspect of adoption in salvation as well—God makes every new believer his child through their faith in Jesus. It is familial adoption.

> To all who did receive him, who believed in his name, **he gave the right to become children of God** (John 1:12).

> In Christ Jesus you are all sons of God, through faith (Galatians 3:26).

Inheritance

In the New Testament, there is a second meaning to adoption. Not only is a spiritual newborn baby transferred into God's family, but he or she is also given the full rights as an adult. This is positional adoption.

In the Greco-Roman world (in which the New Testament was written and understood), a natural-born son would have to be legally adopted by his father to receive the full privileges and rights as a son. This usually happened at a special ceremony between the ages of twelve and fifteen (much like a Jewish *bar-mitzvah*). Until that point, even biological sons had only the rights of slaves or servants. When a person is born again (regeneration), however, he or she is not only adopted into God's family but also immediately receives the full rights as a son.[25]

> For all who are led by the Spirit of God are sons of God. For you did not receive the spirit of slavery to fall back into fear, but **you have received the Spirit of adoption** as sons, by whom we cry, Abba! Father! The Spirit himself bears witness with our spirit that **we are children of God, and if children, then heirs**—heirs of God and fellow heirs with Christ, provided we suffer with him in order that we may also be glorified with him (Romans 8:14-17).

Citizenship

Another aspect of adoption is that we gain new citizenship as well. By adopting us into his family and giving us the full rights, privileges, and responsibilities as adult sons, God also gives us full citizenship into the church and, eventually, into Jesus' kingdom when he comes to reign.

---

[25] In the ancient world, daughters never received those rights or inheritance, so the New Testament always calls us sons, regardless of our gender, to show that both male and female believers receive these rights equally. This is the point of Galatians 3:28, for instance, where the focus is on who can receive salvation and inheritance—everyone!

This heavenly citizenship is more important than any family, citizenship, or allegiance we can have on earth. We are to prioritize those things that God prioritizes, knowing that we will live into eternity, long after this decaying world is destroyed.

> You are no longer strangers and aliens, but you are **fellow citizens with the saints and members of the household of God**, built on the foundation of the apostles and prophets, Christ Jesus himself being the cornerstone (Ephesians 2:19-20).

> **Our citizenship is in heaven**, and from it we await a Savior, the Lord Jesus Christ (Philippians 3:20).

> He has delivered us from the domain of darkness and **transferred us to the kingdom of his beloved Son** (Colossians 1:13).

> Set your minds on things that are above, not on things that are on earth. For you have died, and **your life is hidden with Christ in God** (Colossians 3:2-3).

SANCTIFICATION

The word sanctify means to set apart, to make holy. In the New Testament, the noun form of the word (*hagios*, ἅγιος) is usually translated saint. This is what Paul called every believer in all his letters.[26] Sanctification is the fulfillment of justification when God declared us completely righteous. In a sense,

---

[26] Sainthood is not limited to a few special people who have done great things for God in the past. Because saint means "holy one," God uses it to refer to every believer from the moment of their salvation.

sanctification is the process by which we *become* what God has already declared us to *be*—full of Jesus' righteousness. God's primary goal for every believer is to become like Jesus, reflecting the original image of God more and more.

> God said, '**Let us make man in our image, after our likeness.**' ... So God created man in his own image, in the image of God he created him; male and female he created them (Genesis 1:26-27).

> Those whom he foreknew he also predestined **to be conformed to the image of his Son**, in order that he might be the firstborn among many brothers (Romans 8:29).

> [You were taught] to put off your old self, which belongs to your former manner of life and is corrupt through deceitful desires, and to be renewed in the spirit of your minds, and **to put on the new self, created after the likeness of God** in true righteousness and holiness (Ephesians 4:22-24).

> Do not lie to one another, seeing that you have put off the old self with its practices and have put on the new self, **which is being renewed in knowledge after the image of its creator** (Colossians 3:9-10).

More specifically, sanctification is a process with three phases—past, present, and future—each one having to do with how we relate to our sin.

Past

Past sanctification is the same as justification. It is that point when God declared us not guilty and removed the penalty of our sin.

Present

Present sanctification is sometimes called progressive sanctification. It is the daily process by which we become a little more like Jesus every day as we study the Bible, pray, obey God, confess our sins, and serve others—as we walk *the path*.[27] This is the purpose of all the commands in the New Testament for Christians. It is through this process that we realize that the power of sin in our lives has been removed, and we are free to live under the guidance of God's Spirit.

Because the Holy Spirit indwells us, no Christian *has* to sin. In fact, if we would constantly submit ourselves to the Spirit, we would never sin again. Unfortunately, we fail at this, constantly wanting to live in our own strength and willpower. Even still, God's power is always available to us and is based solely on our obedience to him and our willingness to let the Holy Spirit lead us.

> **Walk by the Spirit, and you will not gratify the desires of the flesh**. For the desires of the flesh are against the Spirit, and the desires of the Spirit are against the flesh, for these are opposed to each other, to keep you from doing the things you want to do. ... But the fruit of the

---

[27] *The path* is how we describe this process, based on 2 Peter 1:3-8. *The path* will be explained in chapter five.

Spirit is love, joy, peace, patience, kindness, goodness, faithfulness, gentleness, self-control; against such things there is no law. And those who belong to Christ Jesus have crucified the flesh with its passions and desires. **If we live by the Spirit, let us also walk by the Spirit** (Galatians 5:16-17, 22-25).

Let not sin therefore reign in your mortal body, to make you obey its passions. Do not present your members to sin as instruments for unrighteousness but present yourselves to God as those who have been brought from death to life, and your members to God as instruments for righteousness (Romans 6:12-13).

Another term for this present phase of sanctification is discipleship, which is the focus of the second section of this book. There we will take the time to explore and explain this process in much more detail. As we will see, this is a lifelong process that requires both our effort and our will.

Future

One of the great hopes for every believer should be our anticipation of the day that we will be with Jesus. At this time, sin will finally no longer be present with us. This future and final aspect of sanctification is sometimes called glorification because it will take place when we receive our glorified bodies in the resurrection. One of the blessings of this new body will be that we will no longer have our sinful nature.

Even though our glorification does not happen immediately when we believe, it is part of the full sanctification process that begins at that time, and Jesus guaranteed us that he will personally accomplish it fully.

> For this is the will of my Father, that everyone who looks on the Son and believes in him should have eternal life, and **I will raise him up on the last day** (John 6:40).

> Beloved, we are God's children now, and what we will be has not yet appeared; but we know that **when he appears we shall be like him, because we shall see him as he is** (1 John 3:2).

> Behold! I tell you a mystery. We shall not all sleep, but we shall all be changed, in a moment, in the twinkling of an eye, at the last trumpet. For the trumpet will sound, and **the dead will be raised imperishable, and we shall be changed**. For this perishable body must put on the imperishable, and this mortal body must put on immortality (1 Corinthians 15:51-53).

Bringing it all together, an easy way to remember these three phases of sanctification concerning sin is that past sanctification has removed the *penalty* of our sin, present sanctification increasingly removes the *power* that sin has over us, and future sanctification will finally remove the *presence* of sin forever.

SUMMARY

In this chapter we explored at least seventeen different things that occur immediately when a person believes in Jesus for salvation:

1. Purchase (Redemption)—He redeems us from the spiritual slave market.
2. Not for resale—He removes us from the market so that we cannot be sold ever again.
3. Release—He frees us from spiritual slavery so that we may choose whom we will serve: our Savior or ourselves.
4. Remission—He forgives our sin with a legal pardon, making us debt-free.
5. Regeneration—He gives us a new spiritual life, a new birth.
6. Imputation (Jesus to people)—He credits us with Jesus' personal righteousness.
7. Justification—Based on Jesus' righteousness, he legally declares us not guilty of all sin and the punishment that goes with it.
8. Reconciliation—He brings us into a new relationship with him as friends instead of enemies.
9. Indwelling—His Holy Spirit begins to live in us.
10. Sealing—He marks us as God's own possession, perfectly securing us until he comes for us.
11. Spirit baptism—He immerses us into the church, the body of Christ, which we can never leave.
12. Spiritual gifts—He empowers us to live out the Christian life and build up our fellow believers.
13. Illumination—He helps us understand the spiritual truths in the Bible.
14. Adoption—He legally brings us into his family as his children.
15. Inheritance—We receive the full rights and responsibilities as heirs of every spiritual blessing.

16. Citizenship—We become citizens of heaven instead of just citizens of earth.
17. Sanctification—He begins the process in us that changes us from sinners into saints who can faithfully reflect God's image.

In addition to these things, we also learned that God imputed our sin to Jesus when he was on the cross, and he paid the wages of sin so that we do not have to do so. Finally, we discovered that, for everyone who knows Jesus as Savior, God has guaranteed we will all make it into his presence, where he will completely remove our sinful nature, and we will be like him as he has always intended.

STUDY QUESTIONS

1. List all the happenings at salvation that you did not know about before reading this chapter.

2. Which of these is the most special or exciting for you? Why?

3. Which of these do you plan to spend more time studying in Scripture?

4. What is the most important truth, principle, or practice you learned from this chapter? What do you plan to do with it?

CHAPTER THREE

WHAT SALVATION IS NOT

The previous two chapters have attempted to explain what salvation is—what it includes and how to obtain it. This chapter goes in the opposite direction. If salvation can be defined and explained by specific truths and events, then it holds that other things are not part of salvation and may even be contrary to it. To keep matters clear, we will use the term Biblical salvation to distinguish between what we have determined the Bible teaches and the other teachings that appear in this chapter.

Think of all the major teachings about salvation as a pendulum, with Biblical salvation at the center. In this diagram,

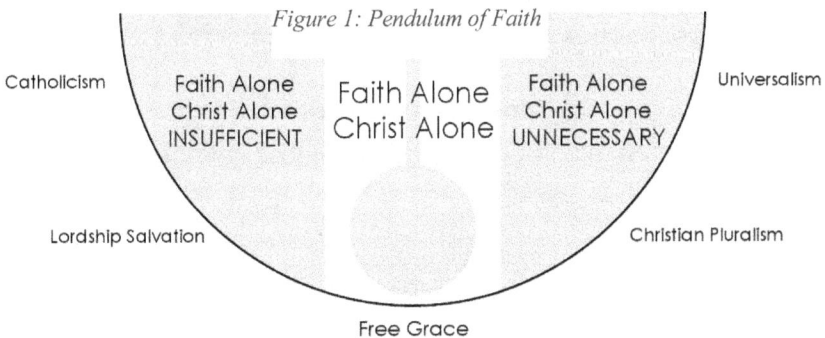

Figure 1: Pendulum of Faith

Catholicism

Faith Alone
Christ Alone
INSUFFICIENT

Faith Alone
Christ Alone

Faith Alone
Christ Alone
UNNECESSARY

Universalism

Lordship Salvation

Christian Pluralism

Free Grace

Biblical salvation is called "Free Grace" and sits under the category of "Faith Alone, Christ Alone."[28]

The shaded categories on either side of Biblical salvation each err in one significant way, holding multiple smaller errors within them. On the left side of the pendulum are those who teach that faith alone in Christ alone is *not enough*. These teachers require people to believe something more or do something in addition to faith before they receive salvation.

On the right side of the pendulum are those who teach that faith alone in Christ alone is *too much*. Rather than adding to the pure gospel, they strip even the basics away from it leaving the gospel empty. In both cases, moving away from Biblical salvation requires changing the gospel message.

FAITH ALONE IN CHRIST ALONE IS INSUFFICIENT

As we have seen in the previous chapters, the apostles were both clear and emphatic that any person can receive salvation but only if 1) they believe in Jesus as God and his death and resurrection as their only means to become right with God, and 2) that salvation is a gift of God's grace.

> For **by grace** you have been saved **through faith**. And this is not your own doing; **it is the gift of God**, not a result of works, so that no one may boast (Ephesians 2:8-9).

> He saved us, **not because of works done by us in righteousness**, but according to his own mercy, by the

---

[28] Pendulum graphic and verbiage used by permission. Paul Miles, *The Pendulum of Faith: Where Do You Stand?* (Lviv, Ukraine: Et Libros, 2019). All rights reserved.

washing of regeneration and renewal of the Holy Spirit (Titus 3:5).

To all who did receive him, **who believed in his name**, he gave the right to become children of God (John 1:12).

Those who say that this is insufficient must add something to the pure gospel—either a prerequisite to faith or something added alongside faith.

Prerequisite to Faith

This teaching is most common in Calvinistic churches and schools and is a direct result of how they understand total depravity. Depravity is a favorite word for some theologians, and how they define it determines much of their belief about salvation. To be depraved simply means to be corrupted. Total depravity, then, means either 1) corruption to the point that a person is completely unable to do any good at all (also called "total inability") or 2) corruption that extends to every part of the person. Calvinism is built on the first definition.[29]

Defining total depravity to mean that there is nothing good in a person or that a person has no ability to do good logically leads to the conclusion that a person cannot respond to Jesus and the gospel. Adherents to this system argue that being "dead in the trespasses and sins" (Ephesians 2:1) completely

---

[29] While not everyone who embraces Calvinism would explain it this way, this is the foundation for the entire doctrine. Changing the definition of "total depravity" automatically changes the other doctrines (or "points") that make up Calvinism. The whole system stands or falls on this definition.

removes all spiritual ability, so that, unless God regenerates them first, they cannot respond to the gospel and exercise faith in Jesus.

> A man is not saved against his will, but he is made willing by the operation of the Holy Ghost. A mighty grace which he does not wish to resist enters into the man, disarms him, makes a new creature of him, and he is saved.[30]

On the surface, this seems to be a God-exalting doctrine. It leaves salvation completely in God's hands to graciously give life and bestow faith on those whom he chooses.[31] Still, beyond the logical issues involved, there are at least three strong Biblical arguments against this teaching.

First, the New Testament never says that faith is a gift that God grants to unsaved people before they can believe in Jesus.[32] To be sure, there are many passages in both the Old and New Testaments that speak to the sinfulness of every person. They say that we would not naturally seek after God on our own

---

[30] Charles Haddon Spurgeon, *Spurgeon at His Best: Over 2200 Striking Quotations from the World's Most Exhaustive and Widely-read Sermon Series* quoted at AZ Quotes (https://www.azquotes.com/quote/606159, accessed 11/17/2019).

[31] This is expanded in the second of the famous "5 Points of Calvinism" — "unconditional election" —the belief that God chose only certain individuals to be saved.

[32] This teaching is usually based on a misunderstanding of one word in the Greek text of Ephesians 2:9. However, even Greek scholars who otherwise believe Calvinistic doctrine reject that interpretation of the passage. Those who continue to point to Ephesians 2:9 to support that faith is a gift for unbelievers do so contrary to the teachings of their fellow Calvinists who understand the original text better.

(Romans 3:10-12) and that we cannot understand spiritual truth without God's help (1 Corinthians 2:14). In order to use these to prove that a person cannot believe without God giving him or her faith, however, overlooks one important point; people today are not without God's help. Jesus promised that the Holy Spirit would have an important ministry toward unbelievers in this world: to convict them about their sin, God's righteousness, and the coming judgment (John 16:8-11). In conjunction with all creation pointing people to God (Psalm 19:1-4; Romans 1:18-21), our conscience convicting us of sin (Romans 2:15), and the preaching of the pure gospel message (Romans 10:14-17), the Holy Spirit calls all people to turn to Jesus and be saved (Acts 17:30–31).

The second problem with this teaching is that the New Testament says that faith always precedes life, not vice versa. In the book written specifically to help bring unbelievers to faith in Jesus, notice the order in which John placed faith and life:

> Now Jesus did many other signs in the presence of the disciples, which are not written in this book; but these are written **so that you may believe** that Jesus is the Christ, the Son of God, **and that by believing you may have life** in his name (John 20:30-31).

According to John, faith comes *before* life, *before* spiritual birth, *before* regeneration. To say that God must give a person spiritual life before they can exercise faith in Jesus is to teach exactly the opposite of the New Testament writers.

The third problem of *prerequisite for faith* teaching is that the New Testament gives only one command for those who are not yet saved: believe.

Then he brought them out and said, 'Sirs, what must I do to be saved?' And they said, 'Believe in the Lord Jesus, and you will be saved, you and your household' (Acts 16:30-31).

For God so loved the world, that he gave his only Son, that **whoever believes** in him should not perish but have eternal life (John 3:16).

For I am not ashamed of the gospel, for it is the power of God **for salvation to everyone who believes**, to the Jew first and also to the Greek (Romans 1:16).

Whoever believes in him is not condemned, but **whoever does not believe** is condemned already, because he has not believed in the name of the only Son of God (John 3:18).

The Bible is clear that everyone who believes will be saved and everyone who does not believe will face eternal punishment for their sin. In both cases, the result is based on whether the person responds to Jesus in faith, not whether God has chosen to give that person faith. One could even argue that God is no longer just if he chooses to withhold faith while at the same time condemning people for not having it. This is not the picture that the Holy Spirit inspired the New Testament writers to portray.

Faith Plus

Another result from teaching that faith alone in Christ alone is insufficient can be that something must be added to faith for a person to be saved. In its broadest sense, this is the foundation of every religion apart from Biblical Christianity.

Any religion that requires a person to do anything—be good enough, follow a specific set of rules or rituals, or even just do your best—is a *faith plus* religion. Biblical Christianity is the only religion that not only offers but requires *faith alone*. The reason for this is simple: as soon as faith is not enough, salvation is no longer a gift—it is earned.

> Now to the one who works, his **wages are not counted as a gift but as his due.** And to the one who does not work but believes in him who justifies the ungodly, his faith is counted as righteousness (Romans 4:4-5).

> For by grace you have been saved through faith. And this is not your own doing; it is the gift of God, **not a result of works, so that no one may boast** (Ephesians 2:8-9).

Any religion or person that requires someone to do something in addition to simple faith in Jesus alone is teaching a false gospel that cannot save. For instance, consider these statements from two major world religions that are often confused with Biblical Christianity (sections underlined for emphasis):

Roman Catholicism

> If any one saith, that nothing besides faith is commanded in the Gospel; that other things are indifferent, neither commanded nor prohibited, but free; or, that the ten

commandments nowise appertain to Christians; let him be anathema [cursed by God].[33]

The grace of the Holy Spirit has the power to justify us, that is, to cleanse us from our sins and to communicate to us 'the righteousness of God through faith in Jesus Christ' and through Baptism. ... Justification is conferred in Baptism, the sacrament of faith.[34]

Mormonism

For we labor diligently to write, to persuade our children, and also our brethren, to believe in Christ, and to be reconciled to God; for we know that it is by grace that we are saved, after all we can do.[35]

Yea, come unto Christ, and be perfected in him, and deny yourselves of all ungodliness; and if ye shall deny yourselves of all ungodliness, and love God with all your might, mind and strength, then is his grace sufficient for you, that by his grace ye may be perfect in Christ; and if by the grace of God ye are perfect in Christ, ye can in nowise deny the power of God...[36]

---

[33] Council of Trent (January 1547), Sixth Session, "Decree on Justification," Canon XIX.

[34] *Catechism of the Catholic Church*, Second Edition, §1987, 1992.

[35] *The Book of Mormon,* 2 Nephi 25:23.

[36] *The Book of Mormon,* Moroni 10:32.

Lordship Salvation

Another label on the left side of the pendulum diagram is Lordship salvation. While it is a much bigger discussion than most people realize, Lordship salvation centers on one key premise that causes it to fit in this category: a person cannot be saved unless they submit themselves to obey Jesus.[37] In other words, according to Lordship salvation teaching, a person must believe in Jesus and his death and resurrection *and also* promise to obey him for the rest of their lives in order to be saved. They may not just call him Savior; they must also call him Lord.[38]

> To put it simply, *the gospel call to faith presupposes that sinners must repent of their sin and yield to Christ's authority.* This, in a nutshell, is what is commonly referred to as lordship salvation [39] (italics original).

There are at least two problems with this teaching. First, it requires something that an unbeliever cannot do—submit to Jesus as Lord before he is saved. It is not surprising that Lordship salvation is held almost exclusively by Calvinists (although not all Calvinists believe it) because it requires God to give the person life, and the faith response is simply an inevitable result of God's work. If God is the one who gives the

---

[37] This concept was popularized (though not invented) by Dr. John MacArthur in his book, *The Gospel According to Jesus* (Zondervan, 1988).

[38] This is an oversimplification of the much bigger topic, but it is the basic element.

[39] "An Introduction to Lordship Salvation," https://www.gty.org/library/Articles/A114/An-Introduction-to-Lordship-Salvation (accessed 11/17/2019).

unbeliever the faith to begin with or changes the person's will so
that they can believe, then it is not a leap to conclude that the
faith God gives will be complete, mature faith, evidenced by
obedience. We have already seen that the Bible does not teach
that God gives faith in order to believe.

The second major problem of Lordship salvation is that it
confuses salvation with discipleship; they confuse *being* saved
with *living out* one's salvation. John MacArthur's website shows
how deceptively easy it can be to arrive at this confusion:

> The gospel that Jesus proclaimed was a call to
> discipleship, a call to follow him in submissive obedience,
> not just a plea to make a decision or pray a prayer. ... He
> taught that the cost of following him is high, that the way
> is narrow and few find it[40] (underlined for emphasis).

It is true that the cost of following him is high, but that is
Biblical discipleship, not Biblical salvation. MacArthur's system
misses the difference between Jesus' context and ours,
specifically that Jesus had not yet died on the cross and been
resurrected, so his message was calling the Jewish people back
to God. They were already in covenant with God but had strayed
away. This is not the same as the gospel message we preach to
unbelievers today.[41]

Since the entire second part of this book will make this
distinction clear, we will not go into it here. Suffice it to say that

---

[40] Ibid.

[41] For more detailed information about the ways God has worked
differently with people throughout time, including before and after the
cross, see *What is Dispensationalism?* (Grace Abroad Ministries, 2018).

salvation and discipleship are clearly distinct throughout the New Testament and any attempt to merge them—as Lordship salvation does—is a grave mistake.

FAITH ALONE IN CHRIST ALONE IS UNNECCESSAY

Whereas the teachings from the left side of the pendulum say that faith alone in Christ alone is not enough, those on the right side take away from the Biblical teaching of what faith alone in Christ alone includes. To review, the gospel message in Scripture is that Jesus is God who became human, died on the cross for our sins, and was resurrected from the dead. Putting all our trust in who he is and what he did for us is the only way to become right with God.

> Then he brought them out and said, 'Sirs, **what must I do to be saved?**' And they said, '**Believe in the Lord Jesus, and you will be saved**, you and your household' (Acts 16:30-31).

> Now I would remind you, brothers, of **the gospel I preached to you**, which you received, in which you stand, and by which you are being saved, if you hold fast to the word I preached to you—unless you believed in vain. For I delivered to you as of first importance what I also received: **that Christ died for our sins in accordance with the Scriptures, that he was buried, that he was raised on the third day in accordance with the Scriptures**... (1 Corinthians 15:1-4).

Every teaching that removes any of these elements changes the gospel message, and the pendulum diagram lists two broad groups in this category: Christian Pluralism and

Universalism. Teachings on this side are more difficult to pinpoint than on the left side of the pendulum because they can include anything that does not contain the Biblical gospel message. If believing in Jesus' death and resurrection is not necessary, what is? The answers fall into two groups: 1) Believe anything you want because it does not matter and 2) Believe in Jesus generically.

Believe Anything (Universalism)

Broadly speaking, universalism teaches that all religions are true and that everyone is on the same path. This is illustrated by the graphic often found on car bumpers all over the United States and other places:

Figure 2: "Coexist" graphic

Along the same lines, Mahatma Gandhi famously stated:

> I came to the conclusion long ago that all religions were true and that also that all had some error in them, and while I hold by my own religion, I should hold other religions as dear as Hinduism. So we can only pray, if we were Hindus, not that a Christian should become a Hindu; but our innermost prayer should be that a Hindu

should become a better Hindu, a Muslim a better Muslim, and a Christian a better Christian.[42]

Depending on the religion one chooses, that path could lead to god/God, mother earth, enlightenment, nirvana, or something else—including the belief that life ceases to exist at all after death (a concept called annihilationism). Typically, those religions that do offer life after death require the person to "be good" or "live well" in this life to earn their place in the next. For example, in Buddhist teachings, *nirvana* is the final state of peace and rest which a person can attain only after going through multiple cycles of birth, life, and death (reincarnation).

More narrowly, the "Christianized" form of Universalism teaches that, in the end, everyone will be saved. They reject eternal punishment, often citing that a God of love could never send anyone to hell. To give just one recent example of this argument, consider these questions and "solutions" offered in the best-selling book *Love Wins*.

> Has God created millions of people over tens of thousands of years who are going to spend eternity in anguish? Can God do this or even allow this, and still claim to be a loving God? Does God punish people for thousands of years with infinite, eternal torment for things they did in their few finite years of life?[43]

[42] Mahatma Gandhi quoted at AZ Quotes, https://www.azquotes.com/quote/376485 (accessed 11/18/2019).

[43] Rob Bell, *Love Wins* (Zondervan, 2001), 2.

Is God our friend, our provider, our protector, our Father—or is God the kind of judge who may in the end declare that we deserve to spend forever separated from our Father?[44]

...given enough time, everybody will turn to God and find themselves in the joy and peace of God's presence. ... To be clear, again, an untold number of serious disciples of Jesus across hundreds of years have assumed, affirmed, and trusted that no one can resist God's pursuit forever, because God's love will eventually melt even the hardest of hearts. ... Which is stronger and more powerful, the hardness of the human heart or God's unrelenting, infinite, expansive love?[45]

In this belief system, salvation is a universal truth because everyone will eventually succumb to God's overwhelming love. This flatly contradicts the Biblical truth that many people have already died apart from a relationship with God through Christ and many others will as well. It denies that the "things [sins] they did in their few finite years of life" are infinite violations of God's perfect image and character. Once we take our last breath in this life, our eternal destiny is secured. There are no more chances in the next life (or lives).

Ultra-Free Grace

As with almost anything else, a good thing can be taken to an extreme and become only a shell of what it once was. This

---

[44] *Love Wins*, 102.

[45] *Love Wins*, 107–109.

is true with free grace theology as well. On our pendulum diagram, *free grace* is the term used for the Biblical position that salvation is a gift from God that we receive through faith—by grace alone, through faith alone, in Christ alone.[46]

In response to the Lordship salvation position that *faith alone* has to include submission to Christ's Lordship over one's life (dedication to obeying Christ) rather than just accepting his death and resurrection on our behalf, a movement arose that attempted to distance itself from the additions that Lordship salvation made to the gospel. However, in doing so, proponents of this new gospel moved the pendulum too far, passing Biblical free grace, and introducing an *ultra*-free grace position that errs in the opposite direction of Lordship salvation. Where Lordship salvation adds to the gospel, ultra-free grace takes away from it.

One of the major proponents of this view was Zane Hodges. He reasoned that, in the gospel of John, the only requirement for salvation is to believe in Jesus. While that sounds the same as the Free Grace position in this book, he explained it to mean that a person does not need to know anything about who Jesus is (God and man) or what he did (death and resurrection), they just need to believe in him. Because of this, Ultra-Free Grace has become known as the *crossless gospel.*

---

[46] These are three of the five statements that summed up the theology of the Reformation in the 16th century. The five phrases in Latin are *sola scriptura, sola gratia, sola fide, solus Christus, soli deo gloria.* In English they mean *Scripture alone, grace alone, faith alone, Christ alone, for the glory of God alone.*

Let me repeat. Neither explicitly nor implicitly does the Gospel of John teach that a person must understand the cross to be saved. It just does not teach this. If we say that it does, we are reading something into the text and not reading something out of it![47]

The simple truth is that Jesus can be believed for eternal salvation apart from any detailed knowledge of what he did to provide it.[48]

Without the name of Jesus there is no salvation for anyone anywhere in our world. But the flip side of the coin is this: Everyone who believes in that name for eternal salvation is saved, regardless of the blank spots or the flaws in their theology in other respects.

Another way of saying the same thing is this: No one has ever trusted that name and been disappointed. In other words, God does not say to people, "You trusted my Son's name, but you didn't believe in his virgin birth, or his substitutionary atonement, or his bodily resurrection, so

[47] Zane C. Hodges, "How to Lead People to Christ, Part 1: The Content of our Message," *Journal of the Grace Evangelical Society 13:2* (Autumn 2000): 7.

[48] Zane C. Hodges, "How to Lead People to Christ, Part 2: Our Invitation to Respond," *Journal of the Grace Evangelical Society 14:1* (Spring 2001): 12.

your faith is not valid." We say that, but God's Word does not.[49]

The Biblical gospel is found in 1 Corinthians 15:3-4 and contains the two necessary elements of Biblical belief: "Christ" (1—who he is) "died for our sins in accordance with the Scriptures...was raised on the third day in accordance with the Scriptures" (2—what he did). Consider this real-life conversation I had with a proponent of this crossless gospel:[50]

> *What does a person have to believe?*
> "Believe in the name of Jesus—John 3:16."
> *But what must I believe?*
> "Believe in his name."
> *Believe what about his name?*
> "Just believe in his name."
> *What about the cross and resurrection? Don't I have to believe that?*
> "No, that is not necessary. Just believe in Jesus."

The problem with Ultra-Free Grace is that it removes so much from the Biblical gospel that it is difficult to distinguish from other world religions. Islam reveres Jesus (*Isa*) as one of their greatest prophets. Does that count as "believing in his name"? Judaism flatly rejects Jesus (Yeshua) as the Messiah, but they readily acknowledge that he existed and made those

---

[49] Zane C. Hodges, "How to Lead People to Christ, Part 1: The Content of our Message," *Journal of the Grace Evangelical Society 13:2* (Autumn 2000): 9.

[50] Adapted from a personal conversation I had with someone who holds to the "crossless gospel."

claims. Does that count as believing in his name? Gandhi was captivated with the Jesus of the Gospels (although, famously, not impressed with Christians) and loved his teaching. Does that mean that Gandhi, who taught that all religions were basically the same, believed in Jesus' name?

It is admirable that these people attempted to take a strong stand against the Lordship salvation additions to the gospel, but they went too far, stripping away the very truths that give the Biblical gospel its power. Ironically, when quoting from their favorite book (the gospel of John), they overlook one key truth that John insisted on teaching:

> Now Jesus did many other signs in the presence of the disciples, which are not written in this book; but these are written **so that you may believe that Jesus is the Christ, the Son of God**, and that by believing you may have life in his name (John 20:30-31).

While it is true that John did not mention the cross in this verse, he clearly wrote that belief in Jesus as the Christ (the Messiah), the Son of God, was required to "have life in his name." By rejecting that a person needs to know even that much about Jesus, the Ultra-Free Grace (crossless) doctrine has rejected the Biblical gospel and preaches a false gospel that does not lead a person to Biblical salvation.

SUMMARY

In this chapter, we explored several teachings that deviate from the Biblical gospel. On the left side of the pendulum are those that add to the gospel—they require something else before a person can exercise faith (Calvinism) or they add works or additional beliefs to the simple faith in who Jesus is and what he did for us (Catholicism, Mormonism, Lordship salvation). On the right side of the pendulum are those that subtract from the gospel—they try to stay within orthodox Christianity but remove the key elements about Jesus and his death and resurrection (Ultra-Free Grace) or they completely leave Biblical Christianity and teach that it does not matter what a person believes because everyone will eventually be saved (Universalism). The Bible is clear that the pure gospel includes who Jesus is and what Jesus did on behalf of all people—nothing more, nothing less. Anything else is a false gospel.

STUDY QUESTIONS

1. Which of these deviations from the Biblical gospel have you heard before? Which are new to you?

2. Which of these seems to be the most dangerous? Why?

3. Could you confidently use Scripture to respond to someone who began to share one of these false gospels with you? If not, which one(s) do you need to prepare for more?

4. What is the most important truth, principle, or practice you learned from this chapter? What do you plan to do with it?

PART TWO
DISCIPLESHIP

CHAPTER FOUR

WHAT IS DISCIPLESHIP?

Make disciples. During the forty days between his resurrection and ascension, Jesus gave his eleven apostles only a few commands that are recorded in Scripture, but Matthew 28:19-20 contains the broad commission that contains the elements of all the others:

> Go therefore and make disciples of all nations, baptizing them in the name of the Father and of the Son and of the Holy Spirit, teaching them to observe all that I have commanded you (Matthew 28:19-20a).

Make disciples is more than "preach the gospel" (Mark 16:15) or "be my witnesses" (Acts 1:8). While it certainly includes those things, it is best explained within its context by the two participles that follow it—"baptizing them" and "teaching them to obey." A disciple is not simply a believer or convert or fan, although he must be all those things. In the fullest sense of the word, a disciple (*mathētēs*, μαθητής) is someone "who engages in learning through instruction from another," who is "constantly associated with someone who has a pedagogical reputation or a particular set of views."[51] In other words, *a disciple is a person who places himself or herself under the instruction of an expert or master with the goal of becoming like the one they are following.*

Finding a modern term to explain this type of relationship is difficult. Words like student and pupil do not go far enough. Decades ago, a good word was apprentice, although today it suffers from the associated concepts of rookie, newbie, novice, or amateur. Many churches find that follower or devoted best express this idea. Surprisingly, even the New Testament writers never used the word disciple outside of the Gospels and Acts, preferring more descriptive terms like holy, saint, or Paul's signature phrase, in Christ. As is evident in this book's title, we will use the terms disciple and discipleship to connect them with Jesus' commission to the apostles.

DEFINING DISCIPLESHIP

Once again, a disciple is a person who places himself or herself under the instruction of an expert or master with the goal of becoming like the person they are following. Notice four key elements that Biblical discipleship requires. First, discipleship is a process that happens to a *person*. While groups and classes can help create environments for discipleship, groups cannot be discipled. Groups may or may not contain Biblical disciples, but having a group meet to discuss Scripture, pray, and fellowship,

---

[51] William Arndt, Frederick W. Danker, and Walter Bauer, *A Greek-English Lexicon of the New Testament and Other Early Christian Literature* (Chicago: University of Chicago Press, 2000), 609 (cited as BDAG).

is not discipleship. Discipleship takes place at the individual, personal level.

Second, discipleship requires a *relationship* with someone else. Discipleship cannot happen in a vacuum. It assumes that the disciple has attached himself to someone else to accomplish something that he could not do on his own. In Jesus' commission, this is found in the words baptizing and teaching.

At its most basic level, water baptism has always been a way for a person to publicly link or identify himself or herself with the specific message or teaching of the group or teacher they are following. For a disciple to be baptized in the name of the Father and the Son and the Holy Spirit means a voluntary submission and identification with God through the person of Jesus as he revealed himself and his apostles recorded in Scripture.

Third, discipleship requires an expert *teacher*. Jesus told the eleven to teach them...everything I have commanded you. Biblical disciples must understand that their pastors, teachers, and professors are not the experts they are following, and those teachers must understand and regularly acknowledge that as well. While Jesus certainly gave these leaders as an important gift to his church (Ephesians 4:11), Jesus himself is the expert Teacher. He is the great Teacher, the Great Shepherd of his sheep. Yes, he uses both human and non-human (the Holy Spirit) agents to accomplish the necessary teaching (1 Corinthians 2:6-16), but Jesus is the one we are following—no one else. The expert we choose to follow matters. Thus, Biblical discipleship is not simply a casual connection to the name of a dead religious leader but a growing understanding of who he is, what he taught, and what he expects from his followers.

Finally, discipleship has a defined *goal* or destination. In the preceding paragraph, a few words are missing from Jesus' command. Not only did he say, "teaching them. . .everything I have commanded"; he said, "teaching them **to observe** everything I have commanded." In other words, Jesus expects his followers to grow in their obedience toward him until they finally become like the Teacher. In theological terms, this is how we become renewed in the image of God. Consider how the apostle Paul used this concept in his teaching.

> Those whom he foreknew he also predestined **to be conformed to the image of his Son**, in order that he might be the firstborn among many brothers (Romans 8:29).

> [You were taught] to put off your old self, which belongs to your former manner of life and is corrupt through deceitful desires, and to be renewed in the spirit of your minds, and **to put on the new self, created after the likeness of God** in true righteousness and holiness (Ephesians 4:22-24).

> Do not lie to one another, seeing that you have put off the old self with its practices and **have put on the new self, which is being renewed in knowledge after the image of its creator** (Colossians 3:9-10).

THE GOAL OF DISCIPLESHIP

Most people do not understand how important and powerful Biblical discipleship is. If believers were fulfilling our commission of becoming Biblical disciples and helping others do the same, most if not all counseling ministries and support groups/programs would be unnecessary. The rooms would be empty because regular, ongoing counseling and support are natural parts of the discipleship process, often disguised as Biblical teaching. The New Testament knows nothing of counseling ministries and support groups, but it knows all about the discipleship process.[52]

So, bringing everything together, we discover that Biblical discipleship is a process and that the goal of this process is individual spiritual growth or maturity—a believer in Jesus becoming more and more like Jesus. In fact, maturity is exactly the analogy the apostles used to explain how the discipleship process works, which we will explore in more detail in chapter seven. There is one more phrase, however, the apostles repeatedly used—almost like a mantra—to sum up the entirety of the process: *know him.*

> **This is eternal life, that they know you** the only true God, and Jesus Christ whom you have sent (John 17:3).

> We know that the Son of God has come and **has given us understanding, so that we may know him** who is true; and we are in him who is true, in his Son Jesus Christ. He is the true God and eternal life (1 John 5:20).

> **...that I may know him** and the power of his resurrection, and may share his sufferings, becoming like him in his death (Philippians 3:10).

---

[52] This is not to say that these ministries are bad or ungodly, simply that if Biblical discipleship were taking place regularly within a local church, the members of that church would not find the need for these other agencies.

In the next chapter, we will see the eight steps that Peter said are necessary to move from being unsaved to a full disciple of Jesus. Interestingly, Peter saturated his teaching with this vital concept of knowing Jesus:

> His divine power has bestowed on us everything necessary for life and godliness **through the rich knowledge of the one who called us** by his own glory and excellence. ... For if these [eight] things are really yours and are continually increasing, they will keep you from becoming ineffective and unproductive in **your pursuit of knowing our Lord Jesus Christ more intimately** (2 Peter 1:3, 8, NET).

> **Grow in the grace and knowledge of our Lord and Savior Jesus Christ.** To him be the honor both now and on that eternal day (2 Peter 3:18, NET).

STUDY QUESTIONS

1. What are the four key elements of Biblical discipleship?

2. Put the definition of a disciple into your own words so that you are sure you can remember, apply, and share it with others.

3. Spend some time meditating on the verses at the end of the chapter about knowing Jesus better. Can you say that this is an important priority in your life right now?

4. What is the most important truth, principle, or practice you learned from this chapter? What do you plan to do with it?

CHAPTER FIVE

THE PATH

As we mentioned at the end of the previous chapter, in the first few verses of his second letter, Peter mentioned eight steps that his readers needed to follow so they would not become "ineffective and unproductive" in their ultimate pursuit: "knowing our Lord Jesus Christ more intimately" (1:8).[53] Technically, only seven of these can be done by believers because the first is faith. According to verse one, this is the same precious faith in "our God and Savior, Jesus Christ" that Peter himself had. It is to this faith that we are to add the other steps.

> For this very reason, make every effort to add to your **faith excellence**, to excellence, **knowledge**; to knowledge, **self-control**; to self-control, **perseverance**; to perseverance, **godliness**; to godliness, **brotherly affection**; to brotherly affection, **unselfish love** (2 Peter 1:5-7).

---

[53] Throughout this book, all quotations from 2 Peter in relation to *the path*, including the names of the eight steps, come from the NET Bible.

Before exploring the details of these steps, we should note two important keys. First, the steps are listed in sequence. Peter was clear that we are to take each step following the previous one. This means that the steps both build on the previous ones and set the foundation for those that follow. Because of the inherent progression of these steps, the sequence cannot be changed, and steps cannot be skipped or ignored if the person is going to attain his goal. *Biblical discipleship follows a specific, God-designed path.*

The second key, as will become clear, is that some of these steps are one-time events while others are repeated. This creates a growth process that we will never complete in this life.

STEP ONE: FAITH

The first step on *the path* of Biblical discipleship (what we will simply call *the path*) is not just the first step; it is the prerequisite.[54] Peter wrote, "Make every effort to **add to your faith**." As noted above, at the outset of the letter, Peter defined the faith that is necessary to begin this process.

> From Simeon Peter, a slave and apostle of Jesus Christ, to those who through the righteousness of our God and Savior, Jesus Christ, have been granted a faith just as precious as ours. 2 Peter 1:1

The faith that Peter had *in* Jesus is the faith necessary to start down *the path* toward Jesus. The goal of *the path* is to

---

[54] Do not confuse this with the prerequisites to faith discussed in chapter three. On *the path*, faith *is* the prerequisite to spiritual growth and maturity. Nothing must come before faith.

know Jesus better and love him more. We cannot do that if we do not know him at all.

The entire first part of this book is dedicated to explaining what faith Peter meant. If you have jumped into this part about discipleship without first reading about salvation, please go back and read the first few chapters. They lay the essential foundation on which Biblical discipleship is built. It is impossible to understand *the path* if we have any confusion about what salvation is and what it is not.

In a sermon he preached years earlier Peter insisted this truth about Jesus: "There is salvation in no one else, for there is no other name under heaven given among men by which we must be saved" (Acts 4:12). This is exactly what Jesus himself claimed: "I am the way, and the truth, and the life. No one comes to the Father except through me" (John 14:6).

This is the gospel that everyone needs to hear. It is the faith that Peter had; it is the faith that he preached; it is the faith upon which the entire *path* stands.

STEP TWO: EXCELLENCE

Excellence is the NET translation of Peter's original word *aretē* (ἀρετή). It is an ancient word going back to the times of Homer and the Greek philosophers. Because of its usage over hundreds of years, the range of meanings built into this word has caused translators and commentators great difficulty as evidenced by the major translations: "moral excellence" (NASB,

NLT, Amp)[55] "virtue" (ESV, N/KJV, ASV)[56] "goodness" (CSB, NIV, NRSV).[57]

Making this even more difficult is the fact that, although it was used regularly throughout Ancient Greek literature, *aretē* occurs only five times in the New Testament—once in Philippians 4:8 and four times by Peter (1 Peter 2:9; 2 Peter 1:3 and twice in 2 Peter 1:5), three of which are in this passage.

Because it is such a rare word in Scripture, we must rely on the context to help us determine which meaning Peter intended. Since Peter wrote later than most of Paul's writings, we can compare the potential meanings of *aretē* with the doctrine found elsewhere in Scripture. A look at reference works is also helpful to determine what meaning Peter could have had in mind.

The basic, standard definition for *aretē* is "uncommon character worthy of praise"[58]; "generally, of a good quality of any

---

[55] New American Standard Bible; New Living Translation; Amplified Bible.

[56] English Standard Version; King James and New King James Versions; American Standard Version.

[57] Christian Standard Bible; New International Version; New Revised Standard Version.

[58] BDAG, 130.

kind"[59]; "the quality of moral excellence."[60] This is the classical Greek usage, especially when related to manhood—"goodness, excellence, of any kind, esp. of manly qualities, manhood, valour, prowess."[61]But, do those definitions fit the Biblical pattern of spiritual growth? Following Peter's sequential steps, are we supposed to immediately add goodness or excellent moral character to our faith before we grow in knowledge, godliness, and the rest? Do our knowledge and self-control build on our goodness or is it the other way around?

The rest of the New Testament teaches that goodness and morality follow knowledge; they do not precede it. Jesus commissioned the apostles to teach their disciples "to obey everything I commanded." Paul wrote that believers are to grow in the knowledge of God and his will so that we can live properly.

> From the day we heard, we have not ceased to pray for you, **asking that you may be filled with the knowledge of his will** in all spiritual wisdom and understanding, **so as to walk in a manner worthy of the Lord, fully pleasing to him**, bearing fruit in every good work and increasing in the knowledge of God (Colossians 1:9-10).

---

[59] Timothy Friberg, Barbara Friberg, and Neva F. Miller, *Analytical Lexicon of the Greek New Testament*, Baker's Greek New Testament Library (Grand Rapids, MI: Baker Books, 2000), 74.

[60] Johannes P. Louw and Eugene Albert Nida, *Greek-English Lexicon of the New Testament: Based on Semantic Domains* (New York, NY: United Bible Societies, 1996), 743. (cited as L-N).

[61] H.G. Liddell, *A Lexicon: Abridged from Liddell and Scott's Greek-English Lexicon* (Oak Harbor, WA: Logos Research Systems, Inc., 1996), 115.

The New Testament pattern is that *right living requires right learning*, not the opposite. We cannot live right if we have not first learned what is right. Thus, human *arete* cannot refer to moral goodness or character as a necessary step of discipleship before knowledge.

Sadly, this is the only option most lexicons offer, which has caused translators much trouble and led commentators to come to a variety of conclusions as to how to interpret and apply it. In many cases, they just assume it means moral goodness or excellent character. Fortunately, this is not the only meaning this ancient word carried. The best option seems to be one of the other uses found in ancient Greek.

The *Theological Dictionary of the New Testament* reveals that there were at least six different legitimate meanings for *arete* (listed as a.-f.). The first three were variations on the definitions found above (a. mastery in a field; b. manliness; c. merit). The following quote discusses the last three options (d.-f.) and offers an important observation about 2 Peter 1:5. It is lengthy and somewhat technical, so I have emphasized the key points of the quote and translated some of the Greek phrases, putting them in brackets.

> At the time of the Sophists the intellectual aspect of the term on the one side, and the ethical, dating from Socrates and Plato, on the other, achieve a prominence unknown in ancient Greece. It is now that the word acquires the particular meaning which becomes predominant and which primarily influences our own impression of it. ἀρετή **becomes a leading tool in the language of Greek moral philosophy in the sense of d. 'virtue.'**...If meaning d. became the main meaning, others

could still maintain themselves and develop alongside it. Religiously it is important that from a very early stage reference could be made to the ἀρετή of the gods. **Later the ἀρετή of a god often came to signify in particular e. his 'self-declaration'** as such. ἀρετή thus came to be linked with -> δύναμις, as a more comprehensive, in relation to powerful divine operation...*ἀρετή* **also means fortune, success (Hom. Od., 13, 45), a good worth seeking, especially in the sense of special prominence among men, i.e., f. 'fame.' It thus comes to be synon. with -> δόξα. The Greek translation of the OT uses it only in this sense...** What both the OT and NT attest is not human achievements or merits but the acts of God. Thus, in the whole of Pauline literature with its wealth of exhortation the word occurs only once and quite incidentally in Philippians 4:8 : ... εἴ τις ἀρετὴ καὶ εἴ τις ἔπαινος, ταῦτα λογίζεσθε [if anything is excellent and if anything is praiseworthy, meditate on these]. Here the proximity of ἀρετή and ἔπαινος [praiseworthy] is perhaps Greek, but hardly their co-ordination. And if the preceding concepts...are co-ordinated with ἀρετή rather than subordinated to it, there is a clear distinction between what Paul has in view and Greek ἀρετή (-> sense f.). The precise understanding depends on whether we think the series has a more secular or a more religious ring. If the latter, then we have an echo of the usage noted in the LXX. ἀρετή is the attitude which the righteous must maintain in life and death. The same is true in relation to the only other passage in which there is reference to human ἀρετή, i.e., 2 Peter 1: : ... ἐπιχορηγήσατε ἐν τῇ πίστει ὑμῶν τὴν ἀρετήν, ἐν δὲ τῇ ἀρετῇ τὴν γνῶσιν. Here a notable formal analogy points us to the secular world, to the sphere of 'virtue.' **Yet it is almost certain that in this passage πίστις is more than the secular parallel ('fidelity') and consequently a similar distinction is likely in the case of ἀρετή. In the same chapter we read just before with reference to God (v. 3) : τοῦ καλέσαντος ἡμᾶς ἰδίᾳ δόξῃ καὶ ἀρετῇ** ["who called us by his own glory and excellence"]. **Here again there is a parallel which points to close contact with the non-Christian world; in both cases the term is to be rendered according to sense e.**[62]

Sense e at the end of the quote refers to the declaration that someone makes about himself (second paragraph of the quote). Bauernfeind concluded that, since *arete* in 2 Peter 1:3 referred to God's self-declaration, it must mean the same thing just two verses later. Does *arete* in verse five, then, mean a new believer's declaration about God or a declaration about himself? The answer is probably a combination of both.

Rather than a reference just to one's own excellent morality, when *arete* was used by God (or even the Greek gods), it was a self-declaration of their own excellencies, moral and otherwise.[63] If we understand *the path's* step of excellence to mean a declaration about oneself, we find that it also best fits

---

[62] Otto Bauernfeind, s.v. ἀρετή in *Theological Dictionary of the New Testament*, ed. Gerhard Kittel, translated by Geoffrey W. Bromiley (Grand Rapids, MI: Wm. B. Eerdmans Publishing Company, 1964), I:458-461.

[63] Even the ancient Greeks recognized that their gods could hardly be considered "moral."

the New Testament teaching of the discipleship process in at least two ways.

First, as discussed in chapters three and four, water baptism has historically been a method of publicly declaring oneself as a follower of a specific religion or teacher. Jesus told the apostles that the first part of making disciples was baptizing them. Thus, water baptism is an essential first step in the discipleship process as the disciple publicly self-declares that he or she is no longer just a *believer* in Jesus but is taking a step to become a *follower* of Jesus as well.

Second, in Romans 6 and 12, Paul taught that spiritual growth follows a believer's decision to dedicate himself or herself to God and his service. Paul commanded believers to "present your bodies as a sacrifice—alive, holy, and pleasing to God" (Romans 12:1). This dedication is an intentional, voluntary act in which the believer declares that he has separated himself to God for everything that the discipleship process entails. As we saw in chapter three, Lordship salvation places salvation and dedication together at the point of salvation, and while some people do dedicate themselves to God immediately after their salvation, the normal New Testament teaching is that dedication comes at some point later.[64]

---

[64] The people for whom dedication comes quickly after salvation are usually those who have grown up in church, hearing the teaching about Biblical discipleship, but who had not yet believed in Jesus for salvation. Unlike many new believers, they do not need a great deal of teaching on this subject right away, so they are able to submit to Jesus as Lord much sooner after they are saved. Regardless, their salvation comes first, then their voluntary dedication to him.

The path is a series of practical steps and commitments we must intentionally and voluntarily make to help us achieve everything that God designed us to be. After salvation, Biblical Christianity requires both faith and work. Unlike Lordship salvation, which puts salvation and discipleship together, Biblical discipleship recognizes that salvation is God's gift to us and discipleship is our lifelong response to that gift. On *the path*, the step of excellence is when the believer makes his or her intentional declaration to identify with and submit to Jesus as Lord or Master, not just Savior.

Compare this to the power steering in a car—the engine provides the power, but the driver is responsible to use the accelerator and brakes and to turn the wheel in the direction he or she wants to go. On *the path*, God provides the power through his indwelling Holy Spirit, but we are responsible for how we steer. Because God released us from slavery (see the section on "Redemption" in chapter two), we are free to steer toward sin and our own desires or toward obedience to the Savior. Salvation is a gift from God but living it out requires our commitment. This was Paul's point when he encouraged the Philippian believers, "Work out your own salvation with fear and trembling, for it is God who works in you, both to will and to work for his good pleasure" (Philippians 2:12-13).

This step may occur in multiple phases and over time as the believer understands that he needs to do this. At the very least, one visible step of this submission to Jesus is obeying him by being baptized (Matthew 28:19). Because Jesus mentioned this specifically as a part of making disciples, it is difficult to see how a person could grow spiritually without being baptized. To ignore his first command, and such a simple one at that, is not an acceptable way to begin *the path* of discipleship.

Another public step of obedience that may fall within excellence may be joining a local church. Many great resources explain why local church membership is vital to the discipleship process, but a short review would include having mature leaders and teachers (Ephesians 4:11; Hebrews 13:17), having a place to exercise spiritual gifts (Ephesians 4:12-16; Romans 12:6-8), and having a place for fellowship and mutual edification with other believers on the same spiritual journey (Colossians 3:15-17).

Most importantly, the step of excellence is the point at which the believer voluntarily and willfully declares that he or she is "all-in" to the discipleship process. As noted above, this is the believer's response to Paul's command to "present your bodies as a sacrifice—alive, holy, and pleasing to God" (Romans 12:1). While it is true that there is a daily aspect to denying ourselves and choosing to follow Jesus (Luke 9:23), a person cannot do this daily if he or she has never made a definitive, one-time commitment to follow Jesus at all. This commitment to all-in dedication is the key element of excellence that may present itself in actions like water baptism and local church membership.

It is important to understand that all-in dedication does not mean that you will have no more questions or doubts or that you finally have all the answers. It does not mean that you will not sin anymore or have no more temptations. It does not even mean that you must go to Bible college or become a pastor or missionary. As you come to know Jesus better and love him more, you will certainly find answers to life's questions. You should choose to sin less. You may even become a pastor or missionary, but that is not what it means.

All-in dedication will result in these new characteristics that will continually increase as you walk *the path*:

- A willingness to submit to God and obey him in everything
- The intentional surrender of all your life to him
- An outside lifestyle showing what is true inside your heart
- The humility to let God do what he wants to do without a fight

Paul summarized all-in dedication in his letter to the Christians in Rome:

We know that our old self was crucified with him in order that the body of sin might be brought to nothing, so that we would no longer be enslaved to sin. For one who has died has been set free from sin. Now if we have died with Christ, we believe that we will also live with him. We know that Christ, being raised from the dead, will never die again; death no longer has dominion over him. For the death he died he died to sin, once for all, but the life he lives he lives to God. So you also must consider yourselves dead to sin and alive to God in Christ Jesus. Let not sin therefore reign in your mortal body, to make you obey its passions. Do not present your members to sin as instruments for unrighteousness, but **present yourselves to God as those who have been brought from death to life, and your members to God as instruments for righteousness** (Romans 6:6-13).

The great gospel music artist, Andrae Crouch, passed away in early 2015. His short song, "My Tribute," is not just a powerful declaration of his own faith but a simple statement of dedication that any believer can make to Jesus today:[65]

> How can I say thanks for the things you have done for me?
> Things so undeserved yet you gave to prove your love for me
> The voices of a million angels could not express my gratitude
> All that I am, and ever hope to be I owe it all to thee
>
> To God be the glory, to God be the glory
> To God be the glory for the things he has done
> With his blood he has saved me
> With his power he has raised me
> To God be the glory for the things he has done
>
> Just let me live my life and let it be pleasing, Lord, to thee
> And if I gain any praise, let it go to Calvary
> With his blood he has saved me
> With his power he has raised me
> To God be the glory for the things he has done!

STEP THREE: KNOWLEDGE

Although the entire discipleship process is about coming to the rich knowledge of Jesus, Peter wrote that we should

---

[65] Andrae Crouch, "My Tribute," © Copyright 1971 Bud John Songs (ASCAP) (admin. by EMI CMG Publishing).

intentionally add knowledge as a part of that process. We gain this knowledge by studying the Bible.

The Scriptures were extremely important to Jesus and his ministry. He quoted them often and taught what God meant when he inspired them to be written. Just before his death, Jesus promised the apostles that the Holy Spirit would remind them of Jesus' teachings (John 14:26), and some of those teachings were included in the New Testament. If we want to know and love Jesus better, we must come to know and love the Scriptures.

> You search the Scriptures because you think that in them you have eternal life; and it is they that bear witness about me (John 5:39).

> Then he said to them, 'These are my words that I spoke to you while I was still with you, that everything written about me in the Law of Moses and the Prophets and the Psalms must be fulfilled.' Then he opened their minds to understand the Scriptures (Luke 24:44-45).

How does Bible knowledge help us be effective and productive in our spiritual lives?

> All Scripture is breathed out by God and profitable for teaching, for reproof, for correction, and for training in righteousness, that the man of God may be competent, equipped for every good work (2 Timothy 3:16-17).

Notice that the Scriptures are useful in at least four ways: to teach us, to reprove us, to correct us, and to train us in righteousness. One person has said that teaching tells us what is right, reproof tells us what is wrong, correction tells us how to be right, and training tells us how to stay right. The ultimate purpose of this training is that we would become equipped to do good works.

> The saying is trustworthy, and I want you to insist on these things, **so that those who have believed in God may be careful to devote themselves to good works**. These things are excellent and profitable for people (Titus 3:8).

> For we are his workmanship, **created in Christ Jesus for good works**, which God prepared beforehand, that we should walk in them (Ephesians 2:10).

Scripture is useful to make us useful. God's goal is to make us like Jesus, and he gave us the Scriptures as the number one tool to accomplish that. Our usefulness to God and this world is directly proportionate to our understanding of Scripture.

We cannot know the Scriptures too much, because we cannot know Jesus too much. When we study the Scriptures properly, they lead us to Jesus and help us become like Jesus. It is not a coincidence that Peter's second letter started with *the discipleship path* and ended with this encouragement:

> Therefore, dear friends, since you have been forewarned, be on your guard that you do not get led astray by the error of these unprincipled men and fall from your firm grasp on the truth. But **grow in the grace and knowledge of our Lord and Savior Jesus Christ**. To him be the honor both now and on that eternal day (2 Peter 3:17-18).

Knowing God is eternal life (John 17:3). It is the ultimate pursuit of our *path*, and part of the process is intentionally reading, studying, and learning the Scriptures so that we can know what he has told us about himself. This takes a commitment to make Bible study a regular and important part of our Christian life. This is the reason that Jesus gave "pastors and teachers" to his church (Ephesians 4:11). While it is true that all believers are to "let the word of Christ dwell in you richly, teaching and admonishing one another in all wisdom" (Colossians 3:16), it is also true that "not many of you should become teachers, my brothers, for you know that we who teach will be judged with greater strictness" (James 3:1). We all need help from fellow believers—including those who are trained in Bible, theology, and the languages in which the Bible was originally written—to help us study and learn more about Jesus from his Word.

STEP FOUR: SELF-CONTROL

If knowledge is studying the Bible, self-control is applying what we learn. One dear lady always liked to say, "Knowledge is the lecture; self-control is the lab work." It is the homework we do after leaving class.

It is one thing to submit to Jesus as Savior (faith); it is another matter to submit to him as Lord or Master (dedication/excellence). Peter wrote that we need to learn what our Lord wants and then put it into action—apply and obey it. The four central steps of *the path* (knowledge, self-control, perseverance, and godliness) create a lifelong loop that will never stop until we finally see him—when we die or he returns for us.

Knowledge is not enough. James reminded us to "be doers of the word, and not hearers only, deceiving yourselves" (James 1:22). Knowing the Bible without obeying it is like eating a meal without digesting it. It offers only a pretend benefit.

Sadly, many believers attempt to jump from faith directly to self-control. They think that once they are saved, they must immediately start being good and doing good works. Sometimes this is an attempt to keep their salvation. Other times they mistakenly think they should repay God in some way for their salvation. No matter their reason, they inevitably fail at "being good" because they never dedicated themselves to God, or they are not in the process of studying and learning the Scriptures. We cannot obey what we do not know. This is why Jesus told his apostles that part of the discipleship process is "teaching them to observe all that I have commanded you" (Matthew 28:20). First, we learn what Jesus wants, then we can begin to apply that in our lifestyles.

There are several ways a person can become better at obeying what he or she is learning from Scripture. First, it is important to remember that the Christian life is designed to be done together. We need to be with each other more than just Sunday mornings. Gatherings like youth group, adult small groups, and ministry teams all provide peer help. Sometimes there is nothing like having a friend in the trenches with you, helping each other, using each other's knowledge, insight, and perspective to supplement our own.

> Two are better than one, because they have a good reward for their toil. For if they fall, one will lift up his fellow. But woe to him who is alone when he falls and has not another to lift him up (Ecclesiastes 4:9-10).

Another practice to help us obey Jesus is to memorize Scripture. Doing homework well requires knowing the lesson, and memorizing Bible verses and passages can be extremely helpful when we do not have the opportunity to open the Bible right away or ask another for help. Psalm 119:11 says, "I have stored up your word in my heart, that I might not sin against you." Every sin is the result of some type of disobedience. Memorizing the Scriptures helps us know Jesus better and love him more. The more we know and love him, the less we will want to disobey him. The less we disobey, the less we sin. Scripture memory leads to sinning less and obeying more.

A third practice is both the simplest and the hardest: just obey. Ultimately, self-control is not the fruit of my will power or fruit of my memory; it is part of the fruit of the Spirit. If the Holy Spirit is not producing self-control in us, it will not happen. There are times when we obey just because we know that it is the right thing to do, even if it is not comfortable or it does not make sense.

Biblical Christianity is a life of faith. The apostle Paul said that "we walk by faith, not by sight" (2 Corinthians 5:7). Some things we will never understand in this life, but we obey them anyway because they help us know him better and love him more. This is the reason knowledge comes before self-control, the lesson before the lab work. We cannot live right if we do not first learn right, and the Holy Spirit is our number one teacher.

Therefore, my beloved, as you have always obeyed, so now, not only as in my presence but much more in my absence, work out your own salvation with fear and trembling, for it is God who works in you, both to will and to work for his good pleasure (Philippians 2:12-13).

Never forget this important point: spiritual growth is God's project. He has given us everything necessary for life and godliness. He is giving us both the desire and the ability to "make every effort" to do our part. Jesus said, "If anyone loves me, he will obey my word...The person who does not love me does not obey my words" (John 14:23-24, NET). Obedience is a natural result of loving Jesus. Trying to obey him without knowing or loving him is just religion, and that is not the goal.

STEP FIVE: PERSEVERANCE

No matter how hard we try, we do not always obey. Applying what the Bible teaches is not always as easy as it sounds. Fortunately, God is ready to forgive us whenever we confess our sin and line up with him again. That does not mean that he ignores our sin or that the consequences of those sins simply disappear. Forgiveness is not the same as condoning sin or being a pushover. God is no pushover, but he does want us to trust him to help us so we do not sin next time, and that is the next step on *the path*.

As we go through life studying the Scriptures (knowledge) and applying them in our daily circumstances (self-control), three things are guaranteed to happen—*tests*, *temptations*, and *trials*. To successfully make it through these situations, we need to persevere, which means choosing to trust God in every situation.

Tests are given by God, like a schoolteacher with a midterm, to show us how well we learned what he taught in the steps of knowledge and self-control. As we choose to trust him, we can pass these faith tests.

> After these things **God tested Abraham** (Genesis 22:1).

> Count it all joy, my brothers, when you meet trials of various kinds, for **you know that the testing of your faith produces steadfastness** (James 1:2-3).

Temptations come primarily from our own sinful nature.[66] In this case, choosing to trust God helps us obey what we know and not yield and fall into sin.

> Let no one say when he is tempted, 'I am being tempted by God,' for God cannot be tempted with evil, and he himself tempts no one. But each person is tempted **when he is lured and enticed by his own desire** (James 1:13-14).

> ...among whom we all once lived in **the passions of our flesh, carrying out the desires of the body and the mind**, and were by nature children of wrath, like the rest of mankind... (Ephesians 2:3).

Trials come primarily from Satan and his sinful world system around us. Sometimes this is called persecution or suffering for being a Christian. There are some Christians who believe that God wants the church to change or fix this world—to make it better before Jesus returns (or so that he *can*

---

[66] It is true that Satan and other people can tempt us as well, but our own sinful hearts tempt us to sin far worse and far more often than all other sources of temptation combined. We truly are our own worst enemies.

return)— but the New Testament gives a different picture. Paul described Satan as "the god of this world" (2 Corinthians 4:4) and "the ruler of the domain of the air" (Ephesians 2:2). John went so far as to say that "the whole world lies in the power of the evil one" (1 John 5:19), and Peter reminded his readers that Satan prowls this world like a lion looking for prey to destroy (1 Peter 5:7). The reason the world persecutes Christians is that it is currently Satan's world, and he hates Christians.

Now it is true that Christians in some parts of the world suffer far more than in other places, but we should never minimize the reality of the constant pressure that does surround us no matter where we live. Perseverance in times of trials and suffering helps us continue to lean into Jesus and not buckle under the pressure.

> Dear friends, **do not be astonished that a trial by fire is occurring among you**, as though something strange were happening to you. But rejoice in the degree that you have shared in the sufferings of Christ, so that when his glory is revealed you may also rejoice and be glad (1 Peter 4:12-13).

Let this be an encouragement to you: *Temptation and discouragement are not sinful.* But, how we respond to them can be. Even Jesus became discouraged at times, and he was certainly tempted throughout his entire life (Hebrews 2:18; 4:14-16; Luke 4:13), but he chose to trust God in everything. Since God is shaping us to become like Jesus (Romans 8:29), we need to choose to trust him as well.

The principle is not "Don't get discouraged"; the principle is, "Don't let discouragement stop you." Instead, let the pressure press you closer to Jesus and what he wants to do in your life. The apostles promised great benefits for those who choose to trust God when we suffer in this life: compassion (James 5:10-11), hope (Romans 15:4), godly character (Romans 5:3-4), and future rewards (Hebrews 10:36).

STEP SIX: GODLINESS

People do not drift toward holiness. Apart from grace-driven effort, people do not gravitate toward godliness, prayer, obedience to Scripture, faith, and delight in the Lord. We drift toward compromise and call it tolerance; we drift toward disobedience and call it freedom; we drift toward superstition and call it faith. We cherish the indiscipline of lost self-control and call it relaxation; we slouch toward prayerlessness and delude ourselves into thinking we have escaped legalism; we slide toward godlessness and convince ourselves we have been liberated.[67]

The tendency to drift has always been part of the Christian life. The first of five warnings that the writer of Hebrews chose to point out to his friends was to "pay closer attention to what we have heard, **so that we do not drift away**" (Hebrews 2:1).[68]

As we obey what we learn in the Scriptures (knowledge and self-control) and choose to trust God in every situation (perseverance), the evil desires and corruption inside us slowly

---

[67] D.A. Carson, *For the Love of God*, Volume 2 (Wheaton, IL: Crossway Books, 1999), Jan. 23rd reading, Kindle.

[68] We will examine all five warnings from Hebrews in chapter 10.

begin to be beaten back as the divine nature grows. It does not happen quickly or suddenly or all at once. This is part of the loop of knowledge leading to godliness (steps 3-6), and most of us are not as far along in the process as we think.

> Through these things he has bestowed on us his precious and most magnificent promises, so that by means of what was promised **you may become partakers of the divine nature, after escaping the worldly corruption that is produced by evil desire** (2 Peter 1:4).

The growth of God's nature in us comes as a result of private worship. Worship means "to render religious reverence and homage"[69] (i.e., to give honor and respect to someone or something). That is close to the original form of the English word, worthship, meaning to acknowledge something or someone's worth.

Worship is an action based on how much we value something. For instance, when we come together to *worship* God, we are saying, "God, you are worth my Sunday morning time, my voice to sing, my mind to study, my money to give, my heart to love and serve my fellow Christians." The worship gathering is worth it because God is worth it.

Private worship (as opposed to public or corporate worship) means that we choose to prioritize God's will—we value God's input—more than just during a worship gathering. Slowly, we grow to honor and respect him in every area of our lives.

---

[69] Dictionary.com, s.v. "worship," accessed 11/19/2019, https://www.dictionary.com/browse/worship.

Godliness, then, is more than just the result of Bible study, obedience, and choosing to trust in difficult times. It is when the divine nature starts to become second nature when we find ourselves *thinking* like Christ, *acting* like Christ, *doing business* like him, *treating others* like him. To put it another way, godliness is when our character, ethics, worldview, and thought patterns accurately reflect Christ. It is at this point in the discipleship process when we are doing more than just *being good*. Instead, we finally begin to experience true spiritual maturity as a regular part of life.

So, if we are trying to become like Jesus, and he is our model for what godliness should look like, we should try to discover what was the number one thing he did to make sure he worshiped privately. How did he intentionally value God's priorities and input? **He prayed.**

Jesus himself **frequently withdrew** to the wilderness and prayed (Luke 5:16).

Now it was during this time that Jesus went out to the mountain to pray, and he **spent all night in prayer** to God. When morning came, he called his disciples and chose twelve of them, whom he also named apostles (Luke 6:12-13).

Surprisingly, there are very few commands in the New Testament to pray. It seems that regular prayer was so ingrained in the early believers that the apostles did not need to remind them to pray, just to pray for specific circumstances.

Is it possible that a man or woman can come to love God for himself alone so that there is a fundamental contentment in life regardless of circumstances? Yes, this is possible, but only through prayer.[70]

Probably the phrase that sums it up the best is what Paul wrote to the Thessalonian believers who were suffering for their new-found faith in Jesus: "Pray without ceasing" (1 Thessalonians 5:17). That may be a well-known verse, but it is actually part of a longer sentence. Even though it spans three verses, it is very short— "Rejoice always, pray without ceasing, give thanks in all circumstances; for this is the will of God in Christ Jesus for you" (1 Thessalonians 5:16-18).

If we were honest, the real issue would not be, "I don't know how to pray." It would be, "It's just not a priority. I don't value it enough to do it." That is why this is a process. You may not be at this step, yet, but know that this is where God wants to bring you, that he is committed to this process, and that he wants you to be committed to it as well.

STEP SEVEN: BROTHERLY AFFECTION

Brotherly affection is the NET translation of *philadelphia* (φιλαδελφία). It is the love or affection someone has for family and close friends. When asked what words or phrases they might use to describe what that looks like in their own families, people often say things like care, protect, watch out for, family bond, best interest, unity, and mutual care.

If all those things can be true in a *human* family, how much more should that be true of the *Christian* family—the

---

[70] Timothy Keller, https://www.bible.com/readingplans/1240-prayer-a-14-day-devotional-by-tim-keller/day/8/ (accessed 2/12/2015).

brothers and sisters who are joined eternally through Jesus' death and resurrection? The bond between believers should be stronger even than between human relatives. Consider how strongly Jesus described this relationship:

> If anyone comes to me and does not hate his own father and mother and wife and children and brothers and sisters, yes, and even his own life, he cannot be my disciple (Luke 14:26).

> Stretching out his hand toward his disciples, he said, "Here are my mother and my brothers! For whoever does the will of my Father in heaven is my brother and sister and mother" (Matthew 12:49-50).

Brotherly affection means building up Jesus' family, the church, the body of Christ. "Encourage one another and build one another up, just as you are doing" (1 Thessalonians 5:11). Giving and serving in our local churches are ways that we can do this, but every believer can and should give and serve, no matter how far they are on *the path*. That does not necessarily mean we are living out brotherly affection. We cannot jump directly from step one (faith) to seven (brotherly affection) just by joining a church ministry team or putting money in the offering.

Peter could have just said "serving" here, but he did not. Brotherly affection is more than serving; it is letting godliness flow through us—Christ's own love for his people—and that cannot happen without working through the previous steps, especially the loop of knowledge through godliness. Brotherly affection is far more than just giving and serving in our church; it is the commitment to ministry as a way of life. When we reach this step, ministry is no longer just a Sunday morning job but a daily mission.

Scripture never commands us to serve on a ministry team; it just says to serve. Ministry teams can be a great way to do that, and they may make sense in the modern local church structure, but they are not the only way to serve. As we choose to look for God's priorities in our lives (godliness), we may begin to ask questions like these: How can I use my time, money, and gifts to build up another Christian today? God, who are you going to put into my life today that I can help walk further down *the path*? Who are you going to put in my mind that I can pray for, call, write a note, or encourage in another way? How can I serve you with this unexpected bonus, commission, or refund?

The best ministry (spiritual gifts, spiritual fruit) comes out of the godly character or Christlikeness that he is developing in us throughout the discipleship process. Ministry is the result of maturity, and significant ministry is the result of significant maturity. We cannot *serve* like him if we are not *becoming* like him. Although every Christian should engage in serving and giving long before this step, it takes some growth and maturity before we serve with the right motivation—Christ's own love.

As we walk *the path*, we discover that anyone can act as a guide for those around them. In fact, as part of our personal growth, we each should intentionally connect ourselves to someone a little bit ahead of us (to help us grow), someone a little bit behind us (so we can help them grow), and someone at the same level (so we can walk together). Once we reach the step of brotherly affection, however, we begin to willingly help other Christians grow (make disciples) as our personal mission and passion.

STEP EIGHT: UNSELFISH LOVE

The final step, unselfish love (*agape*, ἀγάπη), is when we finally put everything together and regularly live the way God designed for us, successfully acting as his ambassadors in this world. It does not mean that we become sinless, but we will find ourselves sinning less. We do not become perfect but are being perfected. We do not become God, but we do become godly.

In his eight steps, Peter made a distinction between brotherly affection and unselfish love. The first is limited to our fellow Christians, but that means that unselfish love goes beyond that. This is where Christ's love that he is developing in us overflows naturally into the rest of the world. Jesus made this connection when he said, "By this all people will know that you are my disciples, if you have love for one another" (John 13:35). One another means fellow Christians, but there is an implication that others will be watching those of us who claim to be Christians. What does that mean?

"Set Christ apart as Lord in your hearts and always be ready to give an answer to anyone who asks about the hope you possess" (1 Peter 3:15, NET). As people see the richness of the truly spiritual life, the satisfaction of life done well, they will ask about it, so Peter said that we should make sure we have an answer.

Christians are never told to argue and debate fine theological points or defend God or the Scriptures with those who do not believe, yet those are some of the biggest reasons many Christians will not share their faith. Instead, we are told to do one thing: have an answer for the hope you possess. If you cannot tell someone about your simple faith in Jesus, how can they believe? "Faith comes from hearing, and hearing through the word of Christ" (Romans 10:17).

In addition to seeing our love for fellow Christians and the church, they should also be able to see our goodness toward our fellow man, even those with whom we may disagree. The apostle Paul wrote, "So then, as we have opportunity, **let us do good to everyone**, and especially to those who are of the household of faith" (Galatians 6:10). While it is true that we should prioritize our spiritual family, that does not give us an excuse for not doing good for others as well. Paul said, "as we have opportunity." The more we prioritize what God does, the more opportunities we will see.

Ideally, this new life of seizing opportunities to do good will result in an attitude of kindness that may cause unbelievers to rethink their own status with God. "Do you presume on the riches of his kindness and forbearance and patience, not knowing that **God's kindness is meant to lead you to repentance?**" (Romans 2:4).

Ultimately, the reason God wants us to reflect Christ in this way is that he has entrusted us with his message of reconciliation (2 Corinthians 5:19) that we are to share with the people of this broken world. May we never forget that God "desires all people to be saved and to come to the knowledge of the truth" (1 Timothy 2:4). There are two ways that a church should grow—internal spiritual growth of the members and external conversion growth as new people are saved. We need to add people to the body, and we need to help them grow and stay healthy. At this step, evangelism becomes a personal mission, rather than just a religious duty.

Reconciliation starts with faith in Jesus, but it is more than that. On those difficult days and weeks when even Christians wonder, "Does any of this really matter to real life?", it is so important to remember that this *is* what really matters. Marriages are healed through Christ; sin is overcome through Christ; tests, temptations, trials are conquered through Christ. It is truly the only story worth telling. In those times when we feel like giving up, we find that it matters most to stay on *the path*. Not only will we grow, but we will be able to help others grow, too, and that completes the circle as we fulfill our commission to *make disciples*.

SUMMARY

The path is where theory finally becomes reality, where our walk with God begins to match our talk about him. *The path* is not just something we *believe*; it is something we *live*. Because of this, each of the eight steps requires a commitment so that we live them out well for the rest of our lives.

Faith—Jesus alone forgives my sin, making me right with God, and starting me on *the path*.

Excellence—I publicly declare that I am all-in; God can do anything he wants—in, through, and with me.

Knowledge—Hearing from God through Bible study will be a top priority for me.

Self-control—I will do whatever it takes to obey what I learn throughout the Scriptures.

Perseverance—I choose to trust God faithfully in every test, temptation, and trial.

Godliness—I will continually pray to align myself with what God values in every situation.

Brotherly Affection—I will give, guide, and serve in my church, helping others along *the path.*

Unselfish Love—My life mission is to help people come to know Jesus better and love him more.

If these things are really yours and are continually increasing, they will keep you from becoming ineffective and unproductive in your pursuit of knowing our Lord Jesus Christ more intimately (2 Peter 1:8).

STUDY QUESTIONS

1. What surprised you most about these steps—the number of steps, the order Peter listed them, something else?

2. What did you expect to find that was not there? What was there that you did not expect?

3. Which step do you think you are stuck on right now? Which commitment do you need to make for a life situation you are facing?

4. What is the most important truth, principle, or practice you learned from this chapter? What do you plan to do with it?

CHAPTER SIX

SOME HELPFUL ILLUSTRATIONS

While studying and teaching *the path*, we discovered that people found it helpful to have other visuals or illustrations to help them understand parts of *the path* better than just the straight informational teaching as in the previous chapter. No illustration is perfect or comprehensive; however, being able to understand the concept in various ways can help make it both more relatable and more practical in your own life and for sharing with others. So, this chapter offers three illustrations to help explain parts or all of *the path*—a water park, DNA, and a simple liquid dispenser with a lid.

WATER PARK

A water park is a fun park, usually with rides, attractions, and restaurants. There is a parking lot and a front door where you must buy a ticket to enter and enjoy what the park offers. While there may be some restrictions on certain rides (for example, "You must be this tall", "You must be able to swim", or "You must be 13 years old or older"), the park itself is open to everyone who has a ticket. The difference between a water park and other amusement parks is that a water park is themed around water, so there are slides that end in swimming pools. Instead of standard roller coasters, the rides may be on a creek or river and will have fountains that splash or shoot water at the guests.

A water park serves as a good illustration of *the path* for many reasons, and each step of *the path* has one or more correlations. Like *the path* discipleship process, a water park is thoughtfully designed to give the best experience to those who want to participate. Some parts are harder and scarier than other parts, but even when it is scary, it has safeguards built-in to keep the participants secure. If someone gets hurt or lost, there is always someone there to help. Further, much like the discipleship process, a water park is best enjoyed with a group of friends—people on the same journey, with the same goals, and the same destination who are excited to experience it together.

Faith

To enter a water park and enjoy anything that it has to offer, a person must purchase a ticket and present it at the gate. In most cases, there is only one entrance and one gate which everyone must use to enter the park. The tickets are not free. While some smaller parks may cost less and larger parks with more rides and attractions may cost more, to get into a water park it always costs something. Even if a person is given a ticket as a gift and they can enter the water park for free, it still cost someone the purchase price of the ticket.

The first step on *the path* is faith. Much like a person cannot experience anything in the water park without presenting a ticket at the gate, a person cannot start *the path* without salvation. Unlike the waterpark, the salvation ticket is available only as a gift from God and only because Jesus already purchased it with his death on the cross. Additionally, there is only one gate; Jesus said, "I am the door" (John 10:9) and "I am the way" (John 14:6). No one can enter the water park or *the path* without having a ticket and using the entrance.

Excellence

Once a person is inside the waterpark, he or she has a decision to make. Now that they are in, what will they do? Some people will enjoy every ride and taste all the food. They will make the most of what the water park has to offer, not content to go home at the end of the day without experiencing everything the ticket provided them.

Others will not do that. One ride that is common to most water parks is the Lazy River. Usually directly after entering the park is a slow-moving, shallow stream. The water park guests can float on little rafts or tubes on the stream that often circles around and through the water park. While on the Lazy River, guests can see the other attractions in the park, but they cannot get to them from the Lazy River. In order to get on the other rides, a person must step out of the Lazy River and intentionally move to another attraction. For various reasons, some people choose to spend an entire day on the Lazy River. They enjoy the fellowship of those around them. They enjoy watching friends and family on the other rides. They may even leave the Lazy River briefly for a snack or meal or break, but instead of getting on another ride, they will go back to the Lazy River.

It could be that they do not think they are skilled enough in swimming to handle certain rides. They may look at how high or how deep some attractions are and let their fears keep them from even trying. As noted above, many are content to float on the Lazy River and never do anything else. In each of these cases, the people have a ticket and came through the entrance—they are *in*—but they are not *all-in* because they have not chosen to engage with everything available.

The second step on *the path* is excellence, the point of decision when a person either commits to be all-in with the spiritual growth process or remains near the entrance (faith) and never experiences everything God has to offer those who choose to know Jesus better and love him more. As we will see in the next chapter, many believers choose to remain spiritual infants, never moving beyond their simple faith, never growing in that faith, and never realizing the abundant life that Jesus offers (John 10:10).

Knowledge

Once a person has committed to participating in the water park activities, the next step is to see what the park has to offer. While they could just wander around the park, seeing whatever was directly in front of them, the best option is to look at a map. There are often maps of the entire park strategically placed at major intersections throughout the park, and printed maps are usually available that people can carry around with them. At any time, a person can look at a map, see where they are in relation to everything else, and decide where they want to go and what is the best route to take. Although it is possible to navigate around the park without a map, their time is much more productive if they know where they are and where they want to be. The decisions they make are based on the information the map provides.

The Bible is the map for the Christian life. It tells disciples what God wants them to experience in this life, what dangers to avoid, and how Jesus and other Christians successfully navigated their lives. Although many Christians stumble through life without direction, Biblical disciples grow stronger and more confident in their faith and life decisions the more time they spend studying the map and making solid choices and decisions based on what the Bible teaches. While a map may be optional for water park guests, the Bible is essential for Biblical discipleship.

Self-Control

Reading the map and seeing everything that the water park has to offer provides little value if people spend all their time with the map but never get on a ride. A person could be an expert on the map—know where every ride is and what type of food each vendor serves—without ever having taken a single bite or sat on even one ride. They could give tours of the park to their friends, pointing out the smallest detail that others may overlook, but they can never speak to their own experience until they get on a ride and eat the food.

Many believers spend time reading the Bible, going to Bible study groups, and listening to Bible programs on the radio, TV, and the internet. They can quote Scripture and give sound Biblical advice when others need to hear it. Yet many of those same people refuse to put it into practice in their own lives. James encouraged his readers to not just talk about their faith but to show it by their obedience. He said that following Jesus means to *do* the Word, not just *listen* to it. Just like finally getting onto a ride at the water park, self-control is when a disciple chooses to obey what he or she is reading in Scripture and apply it to their own lives each day.

Perseverance

For all the fun the water park offers, some things are not much fun. The cold water on every ride makes the water park a perfect activity on a hot, summer day, but hot days also bring long lines of people waiting in the sun to get onto a ride or into a restaurant. As the temperature rises, so do tempers as people push and shove to get past each other. A ride may break down, causing even more congestion for the crowded park. Customers and servers become cross with each other and rudeness reigns. It is enough to cause many people to leave. What was supposed to be fun and exciting turned into frustration and anger.

Perseverance is difficult when things are easy; it seems impossible when things are hard. While Biblical discipleship is not inherently difficult (see the next chapter), it certainly can feel difficult because it takes effort and causes us to stretch and grow. Unlike the water park, perseverance in Biblical discipleship is more than standing in long lines and dealing with difficult people. This is the reason we must learn to trust God in everything as an essential part of the growth process.

Godliness

Like most other things, some water parks are fun one time while others draw people to come back repeatedly. Some people visit their favorite park so often that they begin to recognize the staff. They know the best times to go and when to stay away. They know where the best food is and the best time to go on their favorite rides. They often purchase memberships or annual passes that allow them extra time or give discounts on items that are for sale in the park. These people do not just enjoy the park; they are fans, totally invested in everything they can get out of every visit and eagerly look forward to every time they get to return.

On *the path*, godliness is when the disciple becomes excited about his or her spiritual growth. They had already decided that they were all in (excellence), but the process of learning, obeying, and trusting finally begins sinking deep roots at this stage. They are excited to see their growth. The previous steps are more than just intellectual knowledge as they become part of their normal lives. They look forward to seeing what God is going to do in, through, and with them. Although they cannot tell what is coming next, they know that growth is God's plan and priority for them, and they learn to submit to him increasingly each day.

Brotherly Affection

Water parks need employees to staff the business. They need janitors to clean the grounds, lifeguards to watch over the people in the water, people to manage the rides, and vendors to sell food and merchandise. They need people in the office to take care of the email and money. They need people who can take care of medical needs and people to train new employees. Managing a water park requires having employees working at every level so the guests have a great experience. These employees must be trained and equipped to do their jobs well, and that training must include the knowledge that their job is to serve the guests and their fellow employees.[71] This should help motivate them to be the best employees they can be if they remember the experiences they had when they were guests.

Brotherly affection is the *employee* part of *the discipleship path*. No, not every disciple is required to work for a church or other ministry organization, but the church needs people who have begun to mature in their spiritual lives, who realize that discipleship is more than being a guest at the water park; they need to be actively involved with serving others in the church as well. Fortunately, there is no lack of need. Much like the water park, the church needs janitors, medical staff, executives, teachers, and administrators, as well as those who can show merciful sympathy and those who are multitalented, helping with whatever needs to be done at the moment. Much like the water park staff, disciples need to be trained and equipped for ministry, to know how to use their spiritual gifts, and to remember that they are serving their fellow believers who are also on *the discipleship path.*

Unselfish Love

When someone discovers that a water park has low attendance at certain times of the year, whether they share this information with others depends on their attitude. If they are selfish, they will keep the information to themselves. Why would they share it? If more people come during that time, the park will become crowded. If they are not as selfish, however, they may tell their close family and friends. 'This is exciting! If you

---

[71] In this illustration, guests would be fellow believers and disciples who have not matured to this point yet.

go to the water park at this time, there will be fewer people, and it will be a great experience! If you come together with me, I can even show you the best rides." As much as the water park management wants guests to return, they also want new people to come and enjoy the park. For this, they may design an exciting website or TV commercials, but, most of all, they want their best customers to tell their friends. Why is someone more likely to buy a ticket—because they saw a commercial or because a friend told them about it? Personal invitations from those who are excited are the best advertisement.

On *the path*, the final step is unselfish love, when disciples are no longer concerned only about their own growth or even the growth of their fellow disciples (the people already in the park); now they are actively concerned and engaged in helping unbelievers come to know Jesus and start their own journey on *the path*. God wants every disciple involved in sharing the gospel with unbelievers and to see this as their mission in this world.

> Welcome to "The Best Stuff in the World Today Café"
> We are all believers in a better way
> We were served as customers here not so long ago
> Now we are all waiters, thought you ought to know![72]

---

[72] Take 6, *The Best Stuff in The World Today Café* in *Greatest Hits*, Warner/Reprise Cntry Adv, 1998. CD.

DNA

The double-helix strand of DNA provides an interesting visual for *the path*.[73] DNA is considered the basic code of life. The double-helix strands carry the information that makes each person unique, a creation formed from the DNA of our mother and father. These strands look like twisted ladders, where the rungs are comprised of a combination of four nucleobases connected to sugars and phosphates that make up the outside rails.

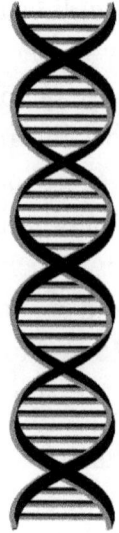

Organizations often use the DNA concept metaphorically to advertise that they are good at something or that a key aspect of their business is so ingrained that it defines them. A quick search for advertising slogans offers several promises that customer service or friendliness, for example, "is in our DNA!"

If a believer is not walking *the path* toward Jesus, he or she is not a Biblical disciple, so *the path* truly "is in the DNA" of a Biblical disciple. Faith and excellence are the two one-time steps necessary to start a person on *the discipleship path*. This could be compared to the two parent DNAs required to create new life. Only after these have been infused into a person does he or she become a genuine disciple of Jesus. At this point, there is a new DNA strand that can begin to develop.

---

[73] As mentioned earlier, every illustration will break down at some point. The goal is not to achieve a perfect one-to-one comparison but rather to offer different perspectives for how to think about and teach *the path*.

The four nucleobases may be represented by the four steps of the internal loop—knowledge, self-control, perseverance, and godliness. These work together in pairs (the first set and second set) that create the rungs by which we walk up *the path*. For the rest of our lives, we continue to complete this loop over and over as we grow in knowledge and let it slowly deepen our character of godliness, each completed loop (like the twist of the DNA strand) bringing us closer to our final goal.

The sugars and phosphates that form the side rails of our *path* DNA are like brotherly affection and unselfish love. Whereas the previous four steps are internal, these final two are external. They slowly rotate around each other and give structure to the entire system.

One similarity between *the path* and a DNA strand is the fact that to develop more outside rails we must develop the inside rungs. In the same way, a disciple cannot have brotherly affection and unselfish love without a strong internal system of knowledge–godliness.

Another similarity is that DNA can get sick and fall apart when it becomes infected with viruses or bacteria—things that do not belong. These can be treated and healed if caught quickly; however, if left to grow, they can become a cancer that requires invasive surgery to cut it out or extreme, painful treatment. Likewise, disciples can become spiritually sick when they do not pay attention to the health of these steps in their lives. They can become so spiritually sick that they can even affect those around them.

If these things are really yours and are continually increasing, they will keep you from becoming ineffective and unproductive in your pursuit of knowing our Lord Jesus Christ more intimately. But concerning the one who lacks such things—he is blind. That is to say, he is nearsighted, since he has forgotten about the cleansing of his past sins (2 Peter 1:8-9).

See to it that no one fails to obtain the grace of God; that no root of bitterness springs up and causes trouble, and by it many become defiled (Hebrews 12:15).

LIQUID DISPENSER

Another helpful illustration for *the path* may be a liquid dispenser. This could be a water jug, thermos, or even a gasoline can. In each case, the purpose of the dispenser is to hold the liquid until it is ready to be used and then be able to dispense it appropriately. While this is a simple concept, there are three key parts that work together much like *the path*—the container, the spout, and the vented lid.

Container

Not all containers are made the same. Their size, material type, and style are all determined by what they are designed to carry. For instance, a gasoline can requires a different material than a water jug because of how gasoline reacts with some materials. Size is an important consideration as well. A personal water jug may hold a gallon (3.8 liters) of water, but that would not be much gasoline, while a 5-gallon (19 liters) gasoline can would be way too much water unless it were for a group of people.

Similarly, each person is designed to carry something specific, namely, the image of God and Christ as a personal temple of the Holy Spirit.

I have been crucified with Christ. It is no longer I who live, but **Christ who lives in me** (Galatians 2:20).

Do you not know that you are God's temple and that **God's Spirit dwells in you?** (1 Corinthians 3:16).

[You were taught] to **put on the new self, created after the likeness of God** in true righteousness and holiness (Ephesians 4:24).

Those whom he foreknew he also predestined to be **conformed to the image of his Son**, in order that he might be the firstborn among many brothers (Romans 8:29).

Through the spiritual gifts distributed by the Holy Spirit (1 Corinthians 12:13) and the maturity developed throughout the discipleship process, every disciple has a specific capacity to do ministry. This is accomplished by the filling of the Holy Spirit, which is how much a disciple is in submission to and controlled by the Spirit at any time. The more we submit, the more he controls, and the more capacity we have for doing his work. On *the path*, this continual choice of submission to his control takes place through the recurring loop of knowledge, self-control, perseverance, and godliness.

We are his workmanship, created in Christ Jesus for good works, which God prepared beforehand, that we should walk in them (Ephesians 2:10).

> Do not get drunk with wine, for that is debauchery, but be filled with the Spirit (Ephesians 5:18).

> Walk by the Spirit, and you will not gratify the desires of the flesh. ... If we live by the Spirit, let us also walk by the Spirit (Galatians 5:16, 25).

Spout

The spout is the means by which what is inside the container comes out. One important point to remember is that the spout does not determine the contents; it only dispenses what is already inside. Sometimes the spout has an open/close switch, sometimes a cap. It can be long or short, wide-mouthed or very narrow. No matter how much of the liquid it dispenses at a time, however, it can only dispense what is already inside the container. This provides two principles. First, whatever goes into the container is what will come out. Second, the spout cannot dispense more than the amount of liquid that is in the container.

This is related to the *principle of the harvest*. A person will always reap *what* he sows, *more than* he sows, and *later than* he sows.

> Do not be deceived: God is not mocked, for whatever one sows, that will he also reap. For the one who sows to his own flesh will from the flesh reap corruption, but the one who sows to the Spirit will from the Spirit reap eternal life (Galatians 6:7-8).

The seeds we plant into our lives—the liquid we put into our container—is what will come out. Unlike a water jug, a harvest will also produce more crops than the seed that was planted. Finally, we harvest later than we sow, and we dispense the liquid in the container at some point after we pour it in.

The spout is brotherly affection and unselfish love. If we are not actively growing and maturing in our knowledge of and love for Christ (the container), when we do attempt to pour out what is inside of us (the spout), it will not be godliness or Christlikeness that comes out. We cannot love our fellow believers and the people of this world with Christ's love if we are not filling ourselves with it. While we can do good things for others, those will not be genuine spiritual ministry if we are not submitted to the Spirit. Only what is inside can come out, which is why brotherly affection and unselfish love always follow the internal maturity steps.

Vented Lid

The third key to this illustration is the vented lid. Most liquid dispensers have a lid or cap of some kind so the liquid in the container does not spill out. We want it to come out of the spout—the right amount, in the right place, at the right time. If the lid is tightened too much or if there is not a small vent hole somewhere on the container, however, little or nothing will come out, even if the container is full. The container needs to be taking in air while it pours out the liquid in order to not create a vacuum inside. In fact, if the walls of the container are thin enough, you can block the vent and watch the sides begin to collapse as the liquid comes out and a vacuum forms. Eventually, the liquid will stop pouring because there is no airflow to help.

In the same way, it is not enough for a disciple to be filled once, then start their ministry of brotherly affection and unselfish love. Much like the Ephesians in Revelation 2, we may keep doing good things, but we will forget why we are doing them because we leave our first love for the Savior. The vent reminds us that the filling—both of knowledge through godliness and Spirit-filling—need to happen regularly if we are going to be able to dispense to others. An "open vent" includes Bible study, prayer (confession, wisdom, help), and submission. Only with this can we be the effective dispensers of God's grace.

> As each has received a gift, use it to serve one another, as good stewards of God's varied grace: whoever speaks, as one who speaks oracles of God; whoever serves, as one who serves by the strength that God supplies—in order that in everything God may be glorified through Jesus Christ. To him belong glory and dominion forever and ever. Amen (1 Peter 4:10-11).

STUDY QUESTIONS

1. Which of these illustrations did you find the most helpful? Why?

2. What would you change to make any of these better so that you can both walk *the path* better and help someone else understand and walk *the path*?

3. What other illustrations can you develop to teach *the path* to someone else?[74]

4. What is the most important truth, principle, or practice you learned from this chapter? What do you plan to do with it?

---

[74] Please send your illustrations to info@theologyisforeveryone.com and let us know if we have permission to use them as we continue to teach *the path.*

CHAPTER SEVEN

THE SPIRITUAL MATURITY CLOCK™

If Biblical discipleship assumes and requires the steps that Peter laid out in *the path*, and if even Jesus knew that this would be a process instead of a one-time event, it is essential to determine if Scripture explains this process in a way that is both clear and practical for every generation. Not surprisingly, the Holy Spirit had the apostles use an analogy that works perfectly across every culture, language, and generation. Anyone can understand easily because it reflects the everyday life of every person who has lived—believers and unbelievers alike. Throughout this book, we have repeatedly used the terms maturity and growth to describe the lives of those who choose to walk *the discipleship path.* The reason is that this is the analogy the apostles used. Physical growth and maturity perfectly mirror the spiritual maturity process.

> ...so that we **may no longer be children**, tossed to and fro by the waves and carried about by every wind of doctrine, by human cunning, by craftiness in deceitful schemes (Ephesians 4:14).

When I was a child, I spoke like a child, I thought like a child, I reasoned like a child. **When I became a man**, I gave up childish ways (1 Corinthians 13:11).

I, brothers, could not address you as spiritual people, but as people of the flesh, **as infants in Christ** (1 Corinthians 3:1).

For though **by this time you ought to be teachers**, you need someone to teach you again the basic principles of the oracles of God. You need milk, not solid food (Hebrew 5:12).

I write to you, **children**, because you know the Father. I write to you, **fathers**, because you know him who is from the beginning. I write to you, **young men**, because you are strong, and the word of God abides in you, and you have overcome the evil one (1 John 2:13-14).

Paul, Peter, John, and the writer of Hebrews all used the stages of physical growth and maturity to illustrate and explain the stages of spiritual growth and maturity. Just as we can often determine a person's stage of physical life, we can often identify their spiritual life stage as well.

From these passages and others, four different life stages become evident. Using the face of a clock and the terms from the above passages, our Spiritual Maturity Clock™ has four quadrants: infant, child, young person, parent.

Humanly speaking, we not only want, but expect, people to develop from one stage to another. From the very first moments after their birth, parents have benchmarks for their infants and children. Their heads, body length, and weight are immediately measured, and those numbers are printed on charts and birth announcements. Parents watch all the percentiles for their height and weight as they grow, often to the point of drawing lines on the walls of their homes and comparing their children's heights. Schools give report cards showing how well children are progressing in their education, as parents expect their children to advance academically.

At the same time, we have a lack of expectations as well. We do not expect a newborn to take out the trash or clean his room. We do not expect a toddler or elementary student to get a job. And rarely are parents excited when they discover that their teenager has become a parent. So, we both expect and do not expect or want certain things based on the stage of life and maturity level of the person we are working with.

The same is true, or at least should be true, spiritually. The apostles expected that they should have been able to talk with these various believers about certain things because they should have grown up by that point. At the same time, they did not expect their readers to be beyond where they should have been, yet they continually pushed and encouraged them to grow. The apostles knew there was a balance, and we know that when it comes to children; we need to understand that in the spiritual life as well.

A clock face helps illustrate this well. The clock reinforces the passage of time as a necessary part of maturity. We often use the phrase "the eleventh hour" to refer to the end of something, including life. Using the numbers one through twelve, we can emphasize milestones or specific points in time that we see growth.

The hands on the clock help as well. The hour hand moves slowly and tells us where we are in the day. We can naturally mark off our four quadrants at 3, 6, 9, and 12. When the hour hand is within a quadrant, that is an indication of our current stage of overall maturity (infant, child, young person, parent).

No matter our *normal* quadrant, however, anyone can have *minutes* or *seconds* in another level at any time. Parents can act like babies, and children can have flashes of brilliance seeming to be older than they truly are. These little moments do not define us, but they are real, even if only briefly.

THREE WARNINGS

Whenever studying what a Biblical disciple should look like and how we should live, there is a temptation to respond in one of three incorrect ways. No matter where we are in this process, the temptations are the same, so it is worth being aware of them before we explore the four stages of spiritual maturity in detail. James' illustration of the mirror is insightful here.

> Be doers of the word, and not hearers only, deceiving yourselves. For if anyone is a hearer of the word and not a doer, he is like a man who looks intently at his natural face in a mirror. For he looks at himself and goes away and at once forgets what he was like. But the one who looks into the perfect law, the law of liberty, and perseveres, being no hearer who forgets but a doer who acts, he will be blessed in his doing (James 1:22-25).

The first temptation is to be dishonest with ourselves. A true disciple of Jesus knows it is essential to look carefully and honestly at oneself if he or she is going to mature properly. There are numerous benchmarks we can use to help identify places we are stunted, but none of them is helpful if we do not review them. An honest evaluation of where we are in the process is the only way to make sure we are growing the way Jesus intends.

The second temptation is to look at other people. We are often tempted to think, "That person needs to grow up! They are definitely not where they should be. Look at how they…" While that may be true, and, yes, they do certainly need to mature, we must avoid the temptation to point the mirror at other people so we do not have to look at it ourselves. This is the same attitude of self-righteousness that Jesus regularly called out in his most vicious opponents.

The third—and possibly the most insidious—temptation is to jump to conclusions. Looks can be deceiving. As we look at ourselves (and others), there are two ways this can lead us astray.

First, although someone is physically old or big, he or she may not be mature. Something may have stunted their growth along the way. Likewise, just because someone has been saved for a long time, they may not be spiritually mature. There are many Christians who have been believers for a long time, but they never grew up; spiritually, they are still infants or children. *Age does not necessarily indicate maturity.*

Second, the opposite side is true as well. Even adults act like babies or make decisions like children sometimes, even though they are truly mature adults. Likewise, just because one slips in his or her spiritual walk, does not mean that he or she is no longer an adult or parent. *Temporary failure does not indicate complete immaturity.* It can mean immaturity in a specific area, or it can mean that they just slipped on *the path*. In either case, other mature brothers and sisters need to come alongside to help these fallen believers come to repentance and restoration with God and each other.

> Brothers, if anyone is caught in any transgression, you who are spiritual should restore him in a spirit of gentleness. Keep watch on yourself, lest you too be tempted (Galatians 6:1).

THE FOUR STAGES OF SPIRITUAL MATURITY

This section will explore each of the four stages of maturity. Using both the Scriptures and the analogy that is so useful from our daily human experience, it is possible for us to identify where we are in our spiritual growth and discover and take the steps necessary to move to the next stage in our spiritual development. The more mature we become the more we will be able to help others grow as well, fulfilling the Great Commission of not just *being* disciples but *making* disciples.

Infant

The first stage of both physical and spiritual life is infancy. Every human starts here, and every Biblical disciple starts here. We need to be born (or conceived) physically, then we need to be *born again*. In our common usage, an infant (or infancy) refers to the earliest part of a person's life, often including the entire period before we can walk on our own. We also use the term to describe a person or organization that is relatively new to a specific field or industry.

Most people like to be around babies because they are cute and curious. Their wonder at life can provide joy and laughter among those who are further along life's journey. But infants have other, less desirable, characteristics as well. They are messy, selfish, needy, and loud. They consume but do not contribute. They know nothing and are completely dependent on others for even the most basic things. Everything must be done for them; they cannot communicate coherently; they cannot even move from one place to another. This means they require enormous amounts of patience and love.

This is a perfect analogy for a new believer. Consider what the aged apostle John expected from his readers who were in this stage of their spiritual development.

> I am writing to you, little children, because your sins are forgiven for his name's sake. I am writing to you, fathers, because you know him who is from the beginning. I am writing to you, young men, because you have overcome the evil one. **I write to you, children [infants], because you know the Father** (1 John 2:12-13).

Normally, babies know their parents very early on; it is one of the first things they learn. They can recognize their parents' voices (even while still in the womb) and faces and quickly develop a strong bond with their mothers and fathers.

John used two different words for little children in verse twelve and children (or infants) in verse thirteen.[75] The spiritual

---

[75] Some English translations begin verse fourteen with the address to infants, while others put it with verse thirteen. The Greek words *teknia* (τεκνια, verse twelve) and *paidia* (παιδια, verse thirteen) can both refer to infants or young children; the context determines the exact meaning. Since John used both in this passage and since he expected more from

infants in John's audience had not yet had the victories that the young people had seen. They might not have been fully sure if all their sins were forgiven like the other, older children. They certainly did not have the range of experience that the fathers did. They were alive (saved), however, and they knew the Father.

At one point during Jesus' ministry, some parents wanted Jesus to place his hands on their infants and children to bless them, but his disciples thought that protecting him from interruption was more important. Jesus' response gives a key principle about spiritual infancy: "Let the children come to me; do not hinder them, for to such belongs the kingdom of God. Truly, I say to you, whoever does not receive the kingdom of God like a child shall not enter it" (Mark 10:14-15).

For the Jewish people looking forward to Messiah's promised kingdom, Jesus said that entrance into his kingdom was tied to how they received it, or their attitude toward it. For some reason, we have taken the "faith of a child" to mean ignorance or innocence. A person does not have to know anything; they just accept it by faith. That is not true. It may start there, but God wants us to grow in both knowledge and experience; we must not stay ignorant. What a child or infant has is *complete dependence*, and being dependent means coming to grips with our lack of ability. The very thing we often resent about babies—their constant need for help—God says is exactly what he is looking for as an indication of a growing disciple.

---

the *teknia* "little children" than the *paidia* "children," we will distinguish them as "children" and "infants," respectively.

As noted above, infants can be cute and cuddly, but they are also completely self-absorbed; everything revolves around them, regardless of how that affects others. According to Paul, this attitude and the lifestyle that comes from it is a key identifier that helps determine whether a person is a spiritual infant.

> So, brothers and sisters, I could not speak to you as spiritual people, but instead **as people of the flesh, as infants in Christ**. I fed you milk, not solid food, for you were not yet ready. In fact, you are still not ready, for **you are still influenced by the flesh**. For since there is still jealousy and dissension among you, are you not influenced by the flesh and **behaving like unregenerate people**? (1 Corinthians 3:1-3, NET).

Spiritual infants have not grown up yet and are still so immature in the Christian faith that their lives can look just like someone who has not been spiritually born yet, an unbeliever. This means that while they may do the right things sometimes, or maybe even a lot, their priorities and attitudes and worldviews have not changed. Life is still all about them, what they need, what they

Figure 3: The hour hand is in the "Infant" quadrant

want to do. They often still live and talk and act and think as they did before salvation. Their family, friends, neighbors, and co-workers may even be unable to tell they are a Christian if no one tells them.

Infants have placed their faith in Jesus for salvation, but that is just the first step. They have not experienced any intentional growth yet, and their lives usually reflect it. God wants us to grow and mature, but that takes time and nutrition, and just like physical infants need milk, so do spiritual infants. "Like newborn infants, long for the pure spiritual milk, that by it you may grow up into salvation" (1 Peter 2:2). This is not just for infants; we all need to thirst for the Scriptures, but that is all infants *can* do for a while. They do not have the strength or the mobility or the knowledge to do anything else, so they sit and absorb.

There are periods of our lives, both physically and spiritually, where we are called to spend more time listening and learning than doing. If we try to start doing things prematurely, beyond our capacity and capability, we can create a mess for ourselves and others.

Child

In the second stage of physical development, people grow from infants into children. This is a broad term that can include anyone from an infant to fully grown. Even as a fully grown adult, I am still my parents' child, and I am a child of the 1970s and '80s. For this study, we are going to limit child to mean those between a toddler and a teenager, about two to twelve years old.

In each stage of development, people have certain characteristics, needs, and abilities. Children tend to be high energy and loud as they continue their exploration of the world. They begin to walk and talk, awkwardly at first, but with increasing proficiency. Much like infants, though, they are still unable to take care of themselves for the first several years. As time goes on, however, they begin to think deeper, communicate more thoughtfully, argue, and push back against discipline. Childhood is a time where rote memory and careful instruction (some would call this indoctrination) is essential because what they learn at this stage will affect and influence the rest of their lives.

Just like the English word, child, can span from infants to young people, so can *teknon* (τέκνον) and *teknia* (τεκνία), the words the apostles used throughout their writings. While there is some overlap in the following passages, there are also more references to children than infants, which provides several keys to understanding this stage of spiritual development.

First, notice that the apostle Paul gave permission to think and act at whatever stage a person is at; he just did not want us to stop there. "When I was a child, I spoke like a child, I thought like a child, I reasoned like a child. When I became a man, I gave up childish ways" (1 Corinthians 13:11). This is an important point as we deal with both physical and spiritual maturity. It is legitimate to act like infants or children when we are truly infants or children. We should not push ourselves (or others) to grow too quickly. Every teacher knows that pushing a child too hard too fast can cause long-term damage. On the other hand, we should not resign ourselves to stay in infancy or childhood simply because we do not want to put in the hard work of growth. We are to grow as much as we can at each stage, slowly and carefully. On the

Figure 4: The hour hand is in the "Child" quadrant

Spiritual Maturity Clock™, this is represented by the slow, steady movement of the hour hand. It takes a long time to move from one o'clock to eleven o'clock, but it does happen.[76]

Children have childish ways, but as they mature, they should set those aside. In this case, Paul was referring to the Corinthians' understanding of healthy doctrine and their use of spiritual gifts in ministry. Children naturally think at a childish level, so they need to be taught how to think better, and they still need people making some decisions for them. "I used to be, but now I'm not" is every growing disciple's story.[77]

The second key to this stage is that we should be careful about what we allow to influence spiritual children. "Brothers, do not be children in your thinking. Be infants in evil, but in your thinking be mature" (1 Corinthians 14:20). Not only is it proper to be an infant when we are truly infants, but it is also legitimate to remain an infant in some areas. We do not have to (or even want to) experience everything in this world to grow or to help each other grow. In fact, Paul said that we should remain innocent like infants when it comes to evil. At the same time, we must not remain immature in our thinking. We should push on to maturity, and *that* maturity in our thinking should help us avoid those areas that may cause us to lose our innocence toward evil. This is the second time that Paul referred to thinking as a

[76] The illustration does break down here slightly because spiritual maturity is not guaranteed. Spiritual maturity does not always push forward. Sometimes it regresses (like some states in the United States that turn their clocks backward) and stops altogether (like a clock with a dead battery).

[77] Compare this to the blind man's testimony in John 9:25: "One thing I do know, that though I was blind, now I see." What a great witness!

key identifier for the child stage, and that is the first of two areas (thinking and acting) we need to develop to move from spiritual child to young person.

Paul's benchmark for an infant was that we often cannot tell the difference between a spiritual infant (saved but immature) and someone who is not saved at all. Spiritual children are sometimes similar, but their thinking and actions have begun to develop and mature because they have taken the initial steps of obedience in their faith. Baptism and church membership are important first steps that can mark the transition from infant to child but to move into childhood requires a complete dedication to Christ. On *the path*, this is the step of excellence. The third step is knowledge which begins to change our thinking.

> About this we have much to say, and it is hard to explain, since you have become dull of hearing. For though by this time you ought to be teachers, you need someone to teach you again the basic principles of the oracles of God. You need milk, not solid food, for everyone who lives on milk is unskilled in the word of righteousness, since he is a child. But solid food is for the mature, for those who have their powers of discernment trained by constant practice to distinguish good from evil. Therefore, let us leave the elementary doctrine of Christ and go on to maturity... (Hebrews 5:11-6:1).

The writer of Hebrews scolded his readers because they should have been more mature than they were by that point, and he knew they were still immature because they did not have a good understanding of major Christian doctrine. As we saw in chapter five, Bible knowledge is not everything, but it is a key benchmark in spiritual development. If a believer is not studying and learning the Scriptures, he or she cannot mature in their Christian faith. Like a water jug, our capability is partially based on how well we know the Scriptures. We know how important it is to teach our children correctly. There is an entire evil world system that is ready and willing to indoctrinate them in so many areas that are directly against the Biblical worldview, so the teaching we provide (both physical and spiritual children) must be solid.

Again, knowledge is not the final goal. In his Great Commission, Jesus said that we are to teach people to obey. This is *the path* step of self-control. Content and sound doctrine matter, but we must also choose to act on it.

> So we are no longer to be children, tossed back and forth by waves and carried about by every wind of teaching by the trickery of people who craftily carry out their deceitful schemes. But **practicing the truth in love, we will in all things grow up into Christ**, who is the head (Ephesians 4:14-15, NET).

Paul said that we will grow as we practice the truth in love. Of course, that means we not only need to *know* the truth; we must also *obey* it. Children are like little paddle boats, easily tossed around by even the smallest waves, because they lack discernment and strength. Kidnappings are rampant in today's world because some people decide they can just take a child away. This happens to spiritual children, as well, and Paul compared this spiritual disaster to what many people face every year. Thousands of families in hurricane regions of the United

States' east coast, the Caribbean, the Pacific Islands, and other places around the world truly understand how destructive wind and waves can be. It can take years to rebuild what a storm can destroy in a matter of minutes or hours. When we do not teach solid, healthy Biblical truth, we put our children at risk to be destroyed by the "trickery of people who craftily carry out their deceitful schemes." How many spiritual "missing child" notices are out there right now for children who were never given sound doctrine and, as a result, have been carried away by false teaching?

Young Person

It is much more difficult to put an age range on this third life stage. As we grow older, young people seem to be older, too! For our purposes, a young person is someone in their teens to early-twenties. People in this stage are nearly fully grown yet still growing. They become more independent yet are often still volatile in their thinking and actions. They can work and carry more responsibility, think more critically, use humor artfully, hurt or help others with their words and actions, and exert tremendous influence. They still need coaching and ongoing education, however, as they embark on their careers and start their families.

Because of how the apostles frequently compared the various stages, many of the passages for young people are the same as those for infants and children, yet they show three characteristics of the spiritual young person. These are things that infants and children should be growing toward and anticipating in their spiritual development.

I am writing to you, young men, because **you have overcome the evil one**. ... I write to you, young men, because you are strong, and the word of God abides in you, and **you have overcome the evil one** (1 John 2:13-14).

One of the characteristics of a spiritual young person is that they have begun to experience spiritual victories, and they exhibit some spiritual strength. It is part of Peter's step of perseverance. To have a victory or conquer something means that we have faced opposition, done battle of some kind, and won. Spiritually, this means that, by the time we have reached young adulthood, we have faced some spiritual battles and come out victorious.

For we do not wrestle against flesh and blood, but against the rulers, against the authorities, against the cosmic powers over this present darkness, against the spiritual forces of evil in the heavenly places. Therefore, take up the whole armor of God, **that you may be able to withstand in the evil day, and having done all, to stand firm** (Ephesians 6:12-13).

Paul did tell his readers to take up this armor and, later, to put it on. If it is God's armor, how can we take it up or put it on? We do this by submitting ourselves completely to him, resting in him, hiding in him, and trusting in him; then *he* defends *us*. This is what Paul wanted believers to understand. Consider what else the apostles wrote on this same topic.

Paul asked, "If God is for us, who can be against us?" (Romans 8:31) James encouraged, "He gives more grace. Therefore, it says, God opposes the proud, but gives grace to the humble" (James 4:6-7). The order is important here. First, we submit ourselves to God, then we can resist the devil. When we submit to God, we are placing ourselves into his hands, his care, behind his armor. It is only then that we can stand our ground and resist. This is not something we could ever do on our own, but even Satan cannot stand against us when God is standing for us.

Peter quoted the same proverb as James,[78] also in the context of spiritual warfare.

> Clothe yourselves, all of you, with humility toward one another, for God opposes the proud but gives grace to the humble. **Humble yourselves, therefore, under the mighty hand of God** so that at the proper time he may exalt you, casting all your anxieties on him, because he cares for you. Be sober-minded; be watchful. Your adversary the devil prowls around like a roaring lion, seeking someone to devour. **Resist him, firm in your faith...** (1 Peter 5:5-9a).

This is the reason that perseverance requires us to trust God in every test, temptation, or trial. A spiritual battle is one that we cannot win without Christ. It is how Paul could say, "Do not be anxious about anything" (Philippians 4:6) because he chose to trust God in everything. Worry and anxiety (especially when they are chronic) are signs of spiritual immaturity. "Everyone who has been born of God overcomes the world. And this is the victory that has overcome the world—our faith" (1

---

[78] Proverbs 3:34.

John 5:4). So, the first characteristic of a spiritual young person is that he or she has begun to win some spiritual battles.[79]

The second and third characteristics come from 1 Corinthians and have to do with thinking and acting, respectively, building on the previous two stages.

Figure 5: The hour hand is in the "Young Person" quadrant

> Yet **among the mature we do impart wisdom**, although it is not a wisdom of this age or of the rulers of this age, who are doomed to pass away (1 Corinthians 2:6).

The second characteristic is that a spiritual young person displays maturity in their thinking. The rest of 1 Corinthians 2 explores the wealth of spiritual insight that is available to a mature believer contrasted with the lack of insight an unbeliever has.

An unbeliever has no ability to grasp spiritual truth. They can understand the words in the Bible and even mentally acknowledge their truth, but without the Holy Spirit's ongoing work of illumination (see chapter two), they cannot go beyond mental understanding. The truths can never become a part of their lives. This is also evident in Paul's later comparison about thinking like a child versus thinking like an adult (1 Corinthians

---

[79] They certainly do not win every battle. There are still losses, but even a handful of victories shows that they are learning to trust God more and more in their everyday lives.

13:11). This level of mature understanding and thinking is possible only when we "let the word of Christ dwell in" us (Colossians 3:16). On *the path,* this is also when we see godliness—God's values and priorities—beginning to take root in our hearts and minds.

The third characteristic of a young person is reflected in their actions, generally and toward one another.

> So, brothers and sisters, I could not speak to you as spiritual people, but instead as people of the flesh, as infants in Christ. I fed you milk, not solid food, for you were not yet ready. In fact, you are still not ready, for **you are still influenced by the flesh. For since there is still jealousy and dissension among you,** are you not influenced by the flesh and behaving like unregenerate people? (1 Corinthians 3:1-3, NET).

Spiritual young people have matured to the point where they are no longer driven by their flesh[80], like infants, but by the Holy Spirit; they are beginning to act more like Jesus (Galatians 5:16-26), and it is obvious in their interactions with one another. Because infants are naturally selfish and self-centered, there is jealousy and dissension among them. But, with maturity comes brotherly affection, a Spirit-driven love and care for their fellow Christians' growth and well-being. As they mature, young people stop provoking each other toward anger and instead "consider how to stir up one another to love and good works"

---

[80] Paul often used the word flesh to refer to our sin nature. This is because sin needs a body in which to work, so temptation to sin often results in both a physical and spiritual response.

(Hebrews 10:24). They press themselves and call each other to a higher standard.

Parent

The final stage of both physical and spiritual development is the parent or teacher stage. Producing a child does not necessarily make someone a parent. Throughout Western culture we have babies making more babies, but they are not parents by any standard other than biological. On the other hand, we all probably know some great parents who cannot or have chosen not to have children, or they thought they were done but have had to step up and be parents again, often because the baby-makers are not taking responsibility.

Within the concept of spiritual parents, there is naturally a part where we are to make spiritual infants—help people come to know Jesus as Savior and be born again; however, making babies is only one small part of parenting, both physically and spiritually. For this reason, many may prefer the word teacher instead of parent for this stage.

Disciples who reach this parent/teacher stage have invested much time and effort into the study and practice of Scripture, and because of this, they can consume and handle harder and deeper truths. This is exactly where the writer to the Hebrews had hoped to find them.

> For though **by this time you ought to be teachers**, you need someone to teach you again the basic principles of the oracles of God. You need milk, not solid food. ...solid food is for the mature, for those who have their powers of discernment **trained by constant practice to distinguish good from evil** (Hebrews 5:12, 14).

Conceptually, parenting is easy and obvious: take the knowledge and experience we have gained and pour it into someone else. In other words, make disciples. As noted in chapter four, however, we must follow the right expert or teacher. Whereas a maturing young person may say, "Follow me, I know the way!", good parents and teachers have come to understand that we are truly followers of someone else. This final stage of maturity is not about getting people to follow us as much as it is helping others see who they are to follow and how to do it. This is what Paul meant when he wrote, "Be imitators of me" (1 Corinthians 4:16; Philippians 3:17) followed by "Be imitators of me, as I am of Christ" (1 Corinthians 11:1). When pressed further on that, he explained, "Be imitators of God, as beloved children. And walk in love, as Christ loved us and gave himself up for us..." (Ephesians 5:1-2). Paul did not want his readers to imitate him for his own sake or because he was special. He wanted them to imitate or follow him only as far as he was imitating Christ.

Spiritual parents and teachers understand that Christ is the goal. He is our highest pursuit, as Peter wrote when he laid out the steps of *the path*. There is no shortcut or quick path to spiritual parenthood. It takes time, patience, and practice—a continual effort to intentionally loop through the steps of *the path* and finally have the maturity to stop looking and pointing at oneself and instead point others to Christ. It is an attitude that looks beyond one generation and seeks to leave a legacy of disciples. At this stage,

Figure 6: The hour hand is in the "Parent" quadrant

disciples fully engage in Jesus' commission and become disciple-makers. This attitude appears throughout Paul's writings (see Ephesians 4:11-16; Titus 2:1-8). This is when brotherly affection and unselfish love become a way of life, and we spend the rest of our days as our clock creeps toward midnight helping others come to know Jesus better and love him more, the same way we have done.

> What you have heard from me in the presence of many witnesses entrust to faithful men who will be able to teach others also (2 Timothy 2:2).

> Him we proclaim, warning everyone and teaching everyone with all wisdom, that we may present everyone mature in Christ (Colossians 1:28).

STUDY QUESTIONS

1. Take some time to think through the characteristics of each stage of maturity and then summarize them in your own words.

2. Based on those characteristics, honestly evaluate yourself. Which stage do you think you are in (the hour hand, not just where you are this minute)?

3. Based on the explanations in this chapter, what do you need to focus on to take your next step toward spiritual maturity?

4. What is the most important truth, principle, or practice you learned from this chapter? What do you plan to do with it?

CHAPTER EIGHT

THE CHARACTERISTICS OF A DISCIPLE

At the end of this work, there is a selected bibliography including some of the best resources that address Biblical discipleship. Of these, the highest recommendations go to Dwight Pentecost's *Design for Discipleship* and Robert Coleman's *The Master Plan of Discipleship*. Their strength is that they attempt to explain what a well-rounded Biblical disciple should look like, rather than focusing on only certain aspects of a godly life. They also have the exceptionally rare qualities of being easy to understand and thoroughly Biblical. This chapter attempts to follow the pattern of these books in outlining what life should look like as a result of choosing to walk *the path* and understand the Spiritual Maturity Clock™.

AN ANALOGY

Sadly, Christians are often the worst advertisement for Christianity. This is not because they are bad people; it is for two reasons. Consider an analogy to shopping for something. In this analogy, the product is Biblical Christianity. First, most Christians know almost nothing about the product. When it comes to salvation, the only thing many Christians know is that it is cheap (just say a prayer) and it is a great value (get out of hell into heaven). Second, most Christians have not spent much time engaged with the product. Many Christians are simply saved sinners, thoroughly carnal (spiritual infants), with no urge or desire to mature beyond that. Yes, they may live under the conviction of their conscience and the Holy Spirit, but they do not understand why they feel guilty for doing what they think is natural. They have not engaged enough with the Bible or godly Christians to show them how powerful Biblical Christianity truly is and how their lives could change if they chose to embrace *the path*.

When I am shopping for a product online, one of the places I spend a lot of time is the customer review section. There are usually three types of customer reviews. First is the five-star review. These customers believe that everything is good, nothing is bad. This is the best product they have ever used; everyone should have one of these. The second type is the one-star review. This is the opposite of the five-star. They say that everything about the product is bad; nothing is ever good. Some customers go so far as to say, "I'll never use or buy junk from this brand again." Notice that in both cases, the review is often nothing more than an emotional response which has been influenced by the ordering or shipping process. It may have nothing to do with the actual product at all.

The third type of review is more measured than the first two. These are often longer than other reviews because the customer has taken the time to work with the product. These reviews have been thought through and usually offer both pros and cons of the product rather than being one-sided. The customer may still give a very low or high rating, but it is the review, not the rating, that provides value to those who are looking for information. A two-, three-, or four-star rating with a solid review should carry much more weight than a short, one- or five-star review that offers no real information.

Thinking of genuine Christianity as a "product," we can see that it follows the same pattern. Christianity is often given five stars by new Christians. One reason for this is that they do not know anything about spiritual growth/maturity/discipleship yet because they have not been saved long enough. They do not know the wonders of what they are holding in their hands. On the other hand, they also have not been saved long enough to find the pits of Christianity—the doubts, the prolonged periods of silence from God, conviction for sin, persecution from this world. All of these affect how they would review their Christianity. Because new Christians often feel so good about their newly found faith, they can be some of the loudest evangelists. Their reviews often sound like this: "Great price and really easy to use; I'm definitely sold on it! Get yours today!"

Christianity also gets one-star reviews, and these can be loud as well. Maybe the person has been part of an overbearing, legalistic church for a long time or the only Christians they know are from such churches. They have been inundated with judgmental looks or comments which resulted in a bad attitude toward God or Christianity. This is the concept behind Gandhi's famous quote: "I like your Christ. I do not like your Christians.

Your Christians are so unlike your Christ."[81] In some cases, the people giving Christianity only one star may not even be saved. If they have only heard judgment and never the pure gospel, their judgment may be based on their experience with how they have seen someone else use the product. Another way to think about it is that they were sold a knock-off or a bad imitation, but not true Biblical Christianity.

These one-star reviews often sound like, "This thing hasn't worked right from the first day, and the customer service (i.e., 'professional' Christians, church staff) was awful. They couldn't answer my questions, or they just assumed I was doing it wrong. No one should ever do business with this company, and I'll tell my family and friends to stay away from them!"

As with online shopping for real products, the measured reviews for Christianity are almost always the most accurate and the best. These come from Christians who have been saved long enough to experience both affliction and comfort. They have engaged in the spiritual disciplines and have seen growth in their relationships with God and others as they learned how to walk *the path* well. They have had both good and bad experiences with other customers (fellow Christians), the support staff (pastors, church leaders), and some of the additional products that are offered by the same company (ministries and programs). Compare this hypothetical review from a maturing disciple (a young person or parent) to the one- and five-star reviews above:

[81] Whether Gandhi truly said this or some form of it is debated, but the sentiment is one that should resonate with Biblical disciples as we see the differences between Christ and those who claim to follow him.

The sales staff did over-promise a little bit, but I found that my overall experience with the product made up for the salesperson's general incompetence.

I am convinced that this would benefit everyone, but I also know that many won't be able to get past the long-term costs, the necessary ongoing maintenance, and the steep learning curve.

That said, most of the customer service reps I've talked with have been extremely helpful. Sure, some of them didn't really have a clue, but it wasn't difficult to transfer to someone else who did. There are also a lot of helps from top-level support staff that are available pretty much everywhere. Some of them are even free on YouTube and other places.

Overall, I'm glad that I went in this direction, and I highly recommend it to anyone who really wants to make serious progress in this area. If you want more details or have specific questions, I'm happy to tell you more.

No matter the product under review, who would not be impressed with someone who gave this much thought and time to their review? When the product is Biblical Christianity, these reviews can be written only by true disciples. Therefore, we understand that growing disciples are the best evangelists.

SEVEN CHARACTERISTICS

An examination of Jesus' and the apostles' teachings indicates that there are at least seven characteristics that should mark a growing disciple of Jesus Christ.[82] Because this is a list of ideal expectations—perfect Christlikeness—we should not expect anyone to achieve them flawlessly in this life. These are areas, however, where the young person should find increasing victories, and the parent should be modeling them regularly. They will certainly fail often and may struggle with some of these more than others, but they will be conscious of this and be working to grow in those areas.[83] A Biblical disciple, then:

1. Commits wholly to Jesus and his absolute authority

2. Places self under the authority of Scriptures and submits completely to its teachings

3. Acknowledges Jesus' ownership of all one's possessions

4. Prays without ceasing for self and others

5. Truly and actively loves fellow Christians

6. Introduces the gospel of Jesus to those who do not know him

7. Willingly suffers hatred from the world against a godly lifestyle

---

[82] The following list is adapted from *Design for Discipleship*, in which Pentecost expands some of these into separate characteristics and adds others. The *purpose* is not to replicate his work but to identify those minimum characteristics that naturally result from walking *the path*.

[83] This is a major difference between an infant or child and young person or parent. While they both may struggle with the same immaturities, the more mature will recognize this and be working to grow whereas the less mature will not.

1. Commits Wholly to Jesus and His Absolute Authority

Our ultimate pursuit in this life is to know Jesus better and love him more. Since the first discipleship step after believing in Jesus for salvation is complete dedication (excellence), it follows that a Biblical disciple must be characterized by his or her total commitment and submission to Jesus and his teachings. This is one of the basic components of the Great Commission: "make disciples...teaching them to obey" (Matthew 28:18-19).

But, total commitment to Jesus is more than just obeying what he said; it is a commitment to Jesus as a person. What begins as a relationship with a Savior, then Master/Lord, is supposed to grow into a friendship. The letter of 1 John was written to help believers remain in fellowship, not just servitude, with Christ and with each other. John used the comparison of walking with each other.

> This is the message we have heard from him and proclaim to you, that God is light, and in him is no darkness at all. If we say we have fellowship with him while we walk in darkness, we lie and do not practice the truth. But if we walk in the light, as he is in the light, we have fellowship with one another, and the blood of Jesus his Son cleanses us from all sin (1 John 1:5-7).

Since God is light, we can choose to walk[84] with him in the light, resulting in close fellowship, or walk in the darkness,

---

[84] The Greek word translated walk throughout this passage and much of the New Testament is *peripateō* (περιπατέω). It normally means to walk,

in sin and away from him. The longer we are in the light with him, the more of ourselves we see from his perspective, which should lead us to confess more sin (verse nine), know him better, love him more, and walk even closer to him. This is the practical living out of the knowledge through godliness loop.

In addition to *walking* with him, we will find ourselves *staying* close to him. Twenty-eight times in 1 John we find the Greek verb, *menō* (μένω), which is usually translated abide or remain. Jesus does not want us to just *walk*; he wants us to *abide* with him. This is the same word Jesus used eleven times in John 15:1-16.

> **Abide** in me, and I in you. As the branch cannot bear fruit by itself, unless it **abides** in the vine, neither can you, unless you **abide** in me. I am the vine; you are the branches. Whoever **abides** in me and I in him, he it is that bears much fruit, for apart from me you can do nothing. If anyone does not **abide** in me, he is thrown away like a branch and withers; and the branches are gathered, thrown into the fire, and burned. If you **abide** in me, and my words **abide** in you, ask whatever you wish, and it will be done for you. ... As the Father has loved me, so have I loved you. **Abide** in my love. If you keep my commandments, you will **abide** in my love, just as I have kept my Father's commandments and **abide** in his love. ... You did not choose me, but I chose you and appointed you that you should go and bear fruit and that your fruit

---

walk around but is often used in the metaphorical sense of live. This is how it is used here.

should **abide**, so that whatever you ask the Father in my name, he may give it to you (John 15:4-7, 9-10, 16)

Over time, this becomes a deep, personal, intimate fellowship with Jesus Christ. It becomes almost symbiotic, as we find our source of everything in Jesus, his words, and his love, and they take root in us. Ideally, this will continue to grow until our physical death (or rapture, see chapter ten) when we are finally united with Jesus, perfect for eternity.

One of the places this fellowship and submission to authority can be evident in practice is the local church. Jesus established the church to be the place where believers can learn to love him and each other better, can exercise their spiritual gifts, and can practice godly submission. This is done best through local membership—the act of voluntarily placing oneself under the God-given authority of the church leadership.

Obey your leaders and submit to them, **for they are keeping watch over your souls**, as those who will have to give an account. Let them do this with joy and not with groaning, for that would be of no advantage to you (Hebrews 13:17).

I exhort the elders among you, as a fellow elder and a witness of the sufferings of Christ, as well as a partaker in the glory that is going to be revealed: **shepherd the flock of God that is among you**, exercising oversight, not under compulsion, but willingly, as God would have you; not for shameful gain, but eagerly; **not domineering over those in your charge**, but being examples to the flock (1 Peter 5:1-3).

Because of the immense ministry that church elders work on behalf of the people entrusted to them, submission to their spiritual leadership and authority is one way we can show our submission to Jesus.[85]

2. Places Self Under the Authority of Scriptures and Submits Completely to its Teachings

The second major submission the disciple performs is to the authority of the Bible. Because the Bible is God's Word, it carries some of God's own qualities:

1. It is *inerrant.* The Bible contains no errors of any kind. While many people accuse the Bible of having contradictions or errors, an honest evaluation of each of these proves to be either a misunderstanding of the text or a false charge. The growing disciple must learn how to handle the Scriptures carefully and accurately, which requires increasing hands-on practice of interpreting it literally.[86] Because the Bible is

---

[85] It is true that not all elders lead well and not all churches are Biblically sound. This is not to advocate those who use their leadership positions as dictators over the congregation or to abuse their flock. At the same time, the principles and commands of Scripture do not change simply because some church leaders are bad. Every Christian is responsible for submitting to godly leadership and, whenever possible, finding a church where the leaders are following the principles laid out in Scripture.

[86] This practice is called the "literal grammatical historical hermeneutic," meaning that we interpret each passage 1) literally—its plain, normal, natural sense; 2) grammatically—the rules of grammar allowed by the original language (including all types of metaphor,

inerrant, the more a disciple studies it, the more he or she finds it as trustworthy and true as God himself.

2. It is *infallible.* Being God's Word, the Bible is both true and inherently truth itself, so it is unable to lead someone in the wrong direction when it is interpreted and applied the way God intended (see above). The principle of single meaning is that every passage has only one intended meaning—the meaning God gave it when it was written. While there are principles that can be applied in a variety of ways in each person's life, a passage never means more or less than it has always meant. When we approach the Scriptures in this way, we can be confident that we are being led the right way by God and toward God. Beware of those who teach that the Bible can change its meaning just for you!

3. It is *authoritative.* Almost no one would deny that, if God spoke to them directly, his words would carry his full authority. Yet many people—Christians included—do not hold the same respect for the Scriptures. However, both Paul and Peter clearly believed that the Scriptures are the very words of God, produced by the Holy Spirit (2 Timothy 3:16-17; 2 Peter 1:20-21). Just hours before he was arrested, Jesus told the apostles that the Holy Spirit would be actively involved in helping them remember Jesus' teachings as well as giving them new revelation, and some of those men in that room contributed those

---

analogy, symbolism, etc.); and 3) historically—how the immediate audience interpreted in their culture and situation.

Spirit inspired words to the New Testament (John 14:26; 16:12-15). In order to walk *the path* faithfully, a growing disciple will submit to the words of Scripture as having all the authority of God.

There is nothing more foundational for spiritual growth than correctly understanding the Scriptures. This is the reason that Paul insisted that teaching healthy doctrine and fighting false doctrine is the primary responsibility of church leaders (1 Timothy 5:17; Titus 1:9-11). As disciples grow in their understanding of Scripture, they will gain a correct understanding of God and people, which will increase their ability to live properly (2 Peter 1:3). Studying and memorizing Scripture also helps develop the Biblical worldview necessary for a disciple to navigate this ungodly world, and a life-long commitment to healthy Bible doctrine puts a growing disciple in the position to teach others also.

What you have heard from me in the presence of many witnesses entrust to faithful men who will be able to teach others also (2 Timothy 2:2).

3. Acknowledges Jesus' Ownership of All One's Possessions

Richard Halverson wrote, "Jesus Christ said more about money than about any other single thing because, when it comes to a man's real nature, money is of first importance. Money is an exact index to a man's true character."[87] As a young pastor, Randy Alcorn was shocked to discover how much Jesus talked about money. "How could the Bible's Author...justify devoting

---

[87] Quoted in Randy Alcorn, *Money, Possessions, & Eternity, Revised and Updated* (Carol Stream, IL: Tyndale House Publishers, Inc., 2003), 3.

twice as many verses to money (about 2,350 of them) than to faith and prayer combined? How could Jesus say more about money than about both heaven and hell? Didn't he know what was really important?"[88] Jesus himself gives the reason for this:

> Where your treasure is, there your heart will be also. ... No one can serve two masters, for either he will hate the one and love the other, or he will be devoted to the one and despise the other. You cannot serve God and money (Matthew 6:21, 24).

> Jesus said to his disciples, Truly, I say to you, only with difficulty will a rich person enter the kingdom of heaven. Again, I tell you, it is easier for a camel to go through the eye of a needle than for a rich person to enter the kingdom of God (Matthew 19:23-24).

Unlike every other "god" that we could serve, wealth has a way of grabbing hold of a person's heart and not letting loose. It creates a need for more that can never be satisfied. The extremely wealthy American businessman, John D. Rockefeller, is famously quoted as saying, "How much money does it take to make a man happy? Just one more dollar."[89] For a person whose god is money, there will never be enough.

The apostle Paul went even deeper, getting to the heart of the issue: "**The love of money** is a root of all kinds of evils. It is through this craving that some have wandered away from the

---

[88] Alcorn, 3–4.

[89] AZ Quotes, https://www.azquotes.com/quote/919457 (accessed Dec 6, 2019).

faith and pierced themselves with many pangs" (1 Timothy
6:10). Money itself is not the problem; money is simply a tool
with which we can build or destroy, help or hurt others. It is the
love of money—better known as greed—that leads to many other
evils. Sadly, the devastating effect of greed impacts believers
more than unbelievers. It can result in:

- Unfruitfulness— "As for what was sown among
  thorns, this is the one who hears the word, but the
  cares of the world and **the deceitfulness of riches
  choke the word**, and it proves unfruitful" (Matthew
  13:22).

- Living outside of God's will— "For all that is in the
  world—the desires of the flesh and the desires of
  the eyes and **pride in possessions**—is not from the
  Father but is from the world" (1 John 2:16).

- Following false teachers— "For people will be
  lovers of self, **lovers of money...lovers of pleasure
  rather than lovers of God**, having the appearance
  of godliness, but denying its power. Avoid such
  people" (2 Timothy 3:2, 4-5).

Again, it is important to remember that it is not money
itself that is the problem but the heart that is dedicated to
wealth. For the disciple walking on *the path*, the lure of wealth
can be overcome with a Biblical perspective about wealth: "The
earth is the Lord's, and all it contains, the world, and those who
dwell in it" (Psalm 24:1, NET).

The opposite of greed is not "have no money"; in fact, that
will only intensify the desire for more. Let's compare the two

concepts of greed and give. If greed is the attitude of "I need more," give is the attitude that says, "*You* need it more." Greed says, "This is mine"; give says, "God has entrusted this to me to use for his work."

A good man leaves an inheritance to his children's children (Proverbs 13:22a).

The point is this: whoever sows sparingly will also reap sparingly, and whoever sows bountifully will also reap bountifully. Each one must give as he has decided in his heart, not reluctantly or under compulsion, for God loves a cheerful giver. And God is able to make all grace abound to you, so that having all sufficiency in all things at all times, you may abound in every good work (2 Corinthians 9:6-8).

Let the thief no longer steal, but rather let him labor, doing honest work with his own hands, so that he may have something to share with anyone in need (Ephesians 4:28).

Even further, giving is to become such a way of life for the Biblical disciple that he or she no longer focuses on asking how much they have to give, but rather how many people they get to serve with the funds that God has entrusted them to use in this life. A disciple works to stop seeing himself as an owner and rather as a financial manager of a small part of God's business.[90]

---

[90] Several good books have been written on this by authors including Randy Alcorn, Dave Ramsey, and Larry Burkett, among others.

4. Prays Without Ceasing for Self and Others

Simply stated, prayer is how a human communicates with God. If the relational goal of discipleship is to become friends with God through Jesus (see the first characteristic), regular communication is essential to build and grow that friendship. Since God is a spiritual being and not here with us physically, prayer is out of necessity a spiritual endeavor. While this comes naturally for some people, others have a much more difficult time with it.

Just as there are different types of communication between humans, there are different types between people and God as well. The Scriptures (especially the Psalms) are full of ways that people talked with God. On a positive note, we find prayers of joy, thanksgiving, celebration, and pure wonder. On the other side are prayers that come out of pain, struggle, fear, doubt, and depression. Yet another method is prayer offered on behalf of others (often called "intercession"). All these are genuine types of prayer, and all these are legitimate ways to approach God. The style is less important than the attitude.

The Bible explains that there are a number of reasons to pray. Communication fosters friendship. Another reason, however, is what most people think of first—getting help from God. Many people like to think of 1 Peter 5:7 without realizing that it is the second half of a sentence that begins in verse six.

> Humble yourselves, therefore, under the mighty hand of God so that at the proper time he may exalt you, casting all your anxieties on him, because he cares for you (1 Peter 5:6-7).

Yes, we are to cast our cares on God, and, yes, God does care for us. However, the attitude with which we bring those cares to him is essential. We must humble ourselves under his mighty hand. Bringing our requests to God should not be a demand; we do not place demands on God. Jesus told the apostles that they should begin to make their requests to God based on their relationship with Jesus, that is, as if Jesus himself were asking (John 14:13; 15:7; 16:24). The reason he could guarantee answers to these prayers is that Jesus always wants what the Father wants, and the Father is glorified to do what Jesus asks. Decades later, John clarified for us what it means to pray through our relationship with Jesus:

> This is the confidence that we have toward him, that **if we ask anything according to his will he hears us**. And if we know that he hears us in whatever we ask, we know that we have the requests that we have asked of him (1 John 5:14-15).

How can we know the will of God? By listening to him in the Scriptures and by obeying what we learn. This makes us sensitive to the Holy Spirit's guidance, and the step of godliness makes the divine nature second nature. To quote from chapter five, godliness is when we find ourselves thinking like Christ, acting like Christ, doing business like him, treating others like him. It is when our character, ethics, worldview, and thought patterns accurately reflect Christ.

As this grows, the communication between a Biblical disciple and God should grow as well. They will pray urgently for themselves and others until they understand the meaning of Paul's plea: "Pray without ceasing" (1 Thessalonians 5:17). Jesus encouraged his listeners to persist in prayer on at least one occasion (Luke 11:5-13). Again, the reason for this is not because God demands that we beg him; he does not need to see us cringe in his presence. The reason is so that we remember that we are humbling ourselves before the Almighty God, the Creator of the Universe, the one who deeply cares about each one of his children individually. So, yes, we are to come boldly to the throne of grace for help as often as we need or want (Hebrews 4:14-16), but we are to come humbly as well.

5. Truly and Actively Loves Fellow Christians

On *the path*, brotherly affection is the second to last step. As explained in chapter five, part of the reason for this is that it takes several cycles of the internal loop (knowledge, self-control, perseverance, godliness) before we mature to the place that ministry is more than simple duty. True brotherly affection is Jesus Christ's own love for his people as worked out by his people.

Church membership was suggested as a way for a Biblical disciple to show his or her identification with Christ's people in the step of excellence. When done in a Biblical manner, becoming a member of a local church is a series of formal commitments. The elders commit to lead the people in truth and godliness, and the members commit to minister and build up each other. Brotherly affection is how this happens.

Unfortunately, the term minister is usually applied only to the pastoral staff, as if they are the only ones doing ministry. In fact, far too often, that is true—the congregation expects the pastoral staff to do the ministry. After all, that is what they are paid to do, right? The answer is a resounding *no!* Ministry is the job of every believer, especially those who have chosen to walk *the discipleship path.* The reason for this is that ministry is simply serving fellow believers with the goal of helping them grow and mature in their discipleship journey.

Jesus' commission to his disciples was the command to make more disciples who would make more disciples (2 Timothy 2:2). Biblical discipleship, by its very definition, is a commitment to help people know Jesus better and love him more. This requires discovering the unique ways which we are each designed to serve.

> For by the grace given to me I say to everyone among you not to think of himself more highly than he ought to think, but to think with sober judgment, each according to the measure of faith that God has assigned. For as in one body we have many members, and the members do not all have the same function, so we, though many, are one body in Christ, and individually members one of another. Having gifts that differ according to the grace given to us, let us use them: if prophecy, in proportion to our faith; if service, in our serving; the one who teaches, in his teaching; the one who exhorts, in his exhortation; the one who contributes, in generosity; the one who leads, with zeal; the one who does acts of mercy, with cheerfulness (Romans 12:3-8).

Discipleship is a life of service to God and each other. As godliness begins to change our natural responses to people and situations around us, Biblical disciples exhibit Jesus' love and find ways to preoccupy themselves with making disciples. What may have once been a chore becomes a joy as they see others around them growing from one maturity stage to another. Doing this long enough allows a disciple to not only be a parent but eventually a spiritual grandparent or great-grandparent. This is what the aged apostle John meant when he quietly reflected, "I have no greater joy than to hear that my children are walking in the truth" (3 John 4).

6. Introduces the Gospel of Jesus to Those Who do not Know Him

The last step of *the path* is unselfish love. This moves the growing disciple beyond just the ministry of helping his or her fellow believers grow into a new mission of pointing unbelievers to Jesus. Although Jesus gifted his church with certain people who are to serve as evangelists (Ephesians 4:11), every believer should be willing and able to share their faith in Jesus. From the analogy at the beginning of this chapter, the more mature a disciple grows, the better (more measured and more credible) their public review of Christianity should be.

By his infinite wisdom, God's power to save people is tied directly to the gospel of Jesus. This is the reason it is essential to make sure we share the pure gospel—nothing added, nothing left out. Paul wrote, "I am not ashamed of the gospel, for **it is the power of God for salvation** to everyone who believes, to the Jew first and also to the Greek" (Romans 1:16). A person cannot be saved without the gospel. Later in the same letter, Paul continued,

> How then will they call on him in whom they have not believed? And how are they to believe in him of whom they have never heard? And how are they to hear without someone preaching? And how are they to preach unless

they are sent? As it is written, 'How beautiful are the feet of those who preach the good news!' But they have not all obeyed the gospel. For Isaiah says, 'Lord, who has believed what he has heard from us?' So **faith comes from hearing, and hearing through the word of Christ** (Romans 10:14-17).

Even if our gospel is veiled, it is veiled only to those who are perishing. In their case the god of this world has blinded the minds of the unbelievers, to keep them from seeing the light of the gospel of the glory of Christ, who is the image of God (2 Corinthians 4:3-4).

Personal evangelism—sharing the gospel—is the point at which we apply the truth that full discipleship means becoming a disciple maker. It is as deep in the battle against Satan as we can get in this world as we try to rescue people from hell before they take their last breath in this life. It is actively imparting the truth of Jesus Christ to those who are ignorant of him and his grace because of their spiritual blindness. The great preacher, Charles Haddon Spurgeon, believed this should be the passion for all believers:

> If sinners will be damned, at least let them leap to hell over our bodies. And if they will perish, let them perish with our arms around their knees, imploring them to stay. If hell must be filled, at least let it be filled in the

teeth of our exertions and let not one go there unwarned and unprayed for.[91]

7. Willingly Suffers Hatred from the World Against a Godly Lifestyle

The final characteristic of a Biblical disciple is not a step on *the path* but the attitude of someone who is solidly in the parent/teacher stage, discipling fellow believers and engaging in spiritual battles against those forces that would keep unbelievers away from Christ (Ephesians 6:12; 1 John 5:19). They are beginning to reflect the image of God in this world in a way that cannot be ignored, as they become increasingly "conformed to the image of his Son" (Romans 8:29). Unfortunately, many who truly desire to experience this are not ready for what comes with it—everything that Satan has to throw against them. If we are faithfully reflecting Jesus' character in our lives, we must carefully heed these words.

If the world hates you, know that it has hated me before it hated you. If you were of the world, the world would love you as its own; but because you are not of the world, but I chose you out of the world, therefore the world hates you. Remember the word that I said to you: A servant is not greater than his master. If they persecuted me, they will also persecute you (John 15:18-20).

---

[91] Michael O'Neal, "Spurgeon's Passion for His City" (Mar 29, 2018), https://www.spurgeon.org/resource-library/blog-entries/spurgeons-passion-for-his-city (accessed Dec 8, 2019).

I have said these things to you, that in me you may have peace. In the world you will have tribulation. But take heart; I have overcome the world (John 16:33).

Although he was a Son, he learned obedience through what he suffered (Hebrews 5:8).

Therefore, since we are surrounded by so great a cloud of witnesses, let us also lay aside every weight, and sin which clings so closely, and let us run with endurance the race that is set before us, looking to Jesus, the founder and perfecter of our faith, who for the joy that was set before him endured the cross, despising the shame, and is seated at the right hand of the throne of God. Consider him who endured from sinners such hostility against himself, so that you may not grow weary or fainthearted (Hebrews 12:1-3).

Indeed, all who desire to live a godly life in Christ Jesus will be persecuted (2 Timothy 3:12).

Why would we think that we could go through this life, attempting to reflect Jesus, and not face the same spiritual opposition that Jesus himself faced? Why would we think that the one who tried so desperately to stop Jesus would not try to stop us as well? Why would God have Paul tell believers about the spiritual armor in which we can take refuge against Satan's deadly attacks (Ephesians 6:10-18)?

A certain seminary professor liked to ask his students about the armor of God. "Why did Paul list these only in Ephesians 6? Why not in his other letters? And why at the end?"[92] One answer is found in Paul's instructions in chapter five. What did he encourage the Ephesian believers to do in their wicked, pagan society?

> Let no one deceive you with empty words, for because of these things the wrath of God comes upon the sons of disobedience. Therefore, do not become partners with them; for at one time you were darkness, but now you are light in the Lord. **Walk as children of light** (for the fruit of light is found in all that is good and right and true) and try to discern what is pleasing to the Lord. **Take no part in the unfruitful works of darkness, but instead expose them**. For it is shameful even to speak of the things that they do in secret. But when anything is exposed by the light, it becomes visible, for anything that becomes visible is light. Therefore, it says, "Awake, O sleeper, and arise from the dead, and Christ will shine on you." **Look carefully then how you walk, not as unwise but as wise**, making the best use of the time, because the days are evil (Ephesians 5:6-16).

This is the reason that Jesus was constantly under attack, and it is the same reason that Biblical disciples are under spiritual attack and need God's protection as well: *they expose spiritual darkness*. This contrast between light and darkness is a key spiritual principle that we find especially in John's writings. In these passages, darkness always refers to evil and light always to good or godliness.

---

[92] Paul did mention individual pieces in other places, but there is no more comprehensive listing than Ephesians 6:10-18.

This is the judgment: the Light has come into the world, and people loved the darkness rather than the Light because their works were evil. For everyone who does wicked things hates the Light and does not come to the Light, lest his works should be exposed. But whoever does what is true comes to the Light, so that it may be clearly seen that his works have been carried out in God (John 3:19-21).

This is the message we have heard from him and proclaim to you, that God is Light, and in him is no darkness at all. If we say we have fellowship with him while we walk in darkness, we lie and do not practice the truth. But if we walk in the Light, as he is in the Light, we have fellowship with one another, and the blood of Jesus his Son cleanses us from all sin (1 John 1:5-7).

The more a believer becomes like Jesus, the more he or she will reflect Christlikeness, and the more Satan's world system will respond with hatred and malice. Crimes are often done under the cover of darkness so the criminal can hide. In English, there is a phrase to express shock or amazement when something is done brazenly; we say it is done "in broad daylight." God is light and when we abide in him and walk with him, we will be in his light and, like a mirror, shining his light into this dark, sinful world.

The Scriptures give us two general ways to do this. First, as noted above, we must carefully choose how we live. Our lifestyles will reflect Christ in our speech, decisions, and actions. Second, we must boldly proclaim the gospel to unbelievers.

> Do all things without grumbling or questioning, that you may be blameless and innocent, children of God without blemish in the midst of a crooked and twisted generation, among whom **you shine as lights in the world, holding fast to the word of life**, so that in the day of Christ I may be proud that I did not run in vain or labor in vain (Philippians 2:14-16).

The more we reflect Christ into this world, the more resistance will confront us. If a believer is facing no opposition in their lives at all, one must wonder if they are truly reflecting Jesus. Part of a truly Biblical worldview is the realization that being like Jesus means suffering like Jesus.

SUMMARY

Although God does not expect us to be more mature than we should be at certain stages in our lives, he does want us to mature, to become more like Jesus. This is the reason for spiritual gifts and spiritual leaders—to help us reach what we cannot reach on our own.

> He gave the apostles, the prophets, the evangelists, the shepherds and teachers, to equip the saints for the work of ministry, for building up the body of Christ, **until we all attain to the unity of the faith and of the knowledge of the Son of God, to mature manhood, to the measure of the stature of the fullness of Christ** (Ephesians 4:11-13).

This requires intentional commitments to *the path* and the Spiritual Maturity Clock™. It requires active involvement in a local church, where we can engage in ministry to build up each other. It requires a growing passion for sharing eternal life with those who do not yet know Jesus. And it requires boldly standing up to the spiritual forces of darkness who will stop at nothing to destroy us, our reputation, our testimony, and our influence in this world. Finally, it requires the knowledge that we will stand before God, responsible for our faithfulness or lack thereof in carrying out our commitment, which will ultimately be judged by Christ himself.

In conclusion, a growing disciple takes to heart and life the simple, yet demanding and complex, command: "You shall be holy, for I the LORD your God am holy" (Leviticus 19:2; see also Matthew 5:48; 1 Peter 1:16). No matter where you are on your *path* to spiritual maturity, if you know Jesus as Savior, would you be willing to make this commitment today:

> *This is the type of disciple I want to be for my Savior, and by God's grace I commit to spending the rest of my life doing my part to achieve it.*

STUDY QUESTIONS

1. Of these seven characteristics:

    a. Which one(s) do you experience regular victory in your life?

    b. Which one(s) do you experience nominal or irregular victory?

    c. Which one(s) do you find yourself constantly struggling with?

2. When you share your faith with others, do you give one-star, five-star, or measured reviews? Why?

3. What is the most important truth, principle, or practice you learned from this chapter? What do you plan to do with it?

PART THREE
ETERNAL EFFECTS

CHAPTER NINE

THE ISSUE OF ETERNAL REWARDS

One issue that has not yet come up in this study of spiritual maturity is the issue of rewards. Both the Old and New Testaments are full of promises that God has made to those who remain faithful in their obedience to him. For the nation of Israel, this included big promises such as health and prosperity (Exodus 15:26; Deuteronomy 28). After Israel rejected him as their Messiah, Jesus shifted his discussion of rewards to his future kingdom. For instance, he promised the apostles that they would reign with him in his kingdom (also a great promise of resurrection, Matthew 19:28). As we will see, this promise of future reward for current faithfulness continued into the church.

In examining the Biblical teaching of future rewards, there are a few concerns that must be addressed. The first is whether God offers rewards today at all. Second is whether we should expect or work for these rewards. Third, of course, is what kind of rewards God has promised. This chapter will attempt to answer each of these carefully.

DOES GOD OFFER REWARDS FOR FAITHFULNESS?

The simple answer is yes, he does. The writer of Hebrews thought this was an essential truth that we must believe about God. "Without faith it is impossible to please him, for whoever would draw near to God must believe that he exists **and that he rewards those who seek him**" (Hebrews 11:6). While there are those who argue against the concept of future rewards, when pressed on this issue, the truth is that they are simply uncomfortable with the idea of incentives or bribery for obedience. Of course, when we phrase it that way, all believers would be uncomfortable, but that falls under the second question, should rewards be our motivation for obedience?[93] When faced with the clear Scripture showing that God does indeed offer rewards, they often accept the idea, albeit still uneasy with the concept.

It is essential to understand that this is not a question about salvation. As has been stated many times previously, God never gives salvation in return for anything we could do. Salvation and everything it entails (see chapter two) is a gift based purely on God's grace. Rewards (also called our inheritance), on the other hand, are earned by those who are already saved based on the works we do in obedience to Christ.

---

[93] This is the basic concept that led to the belief in *amillennialism* (no future physical kingdom). Origen and Augustine (fourth century religious leaders), for instance, thought that the concept of rewards and a physical kingdom were too materialistic and chose to spiritualize those passages rather than take them literally. See Gregg R. Allison, *Historical Theology: An Introduction to Christian Doctrine* (Grand Rapids, MI: Zondervan, 2011), 684-8 for more information about how this developed.

This is the whole purpose of the judgment seat of Christ, which we find explained in three passages.

> We make it our aim to please him. For we must all appear before the **judgment seat** of Christ, so that **each one may receive what is due** for what he has done in the body, **whether good or evil** (2 Corinthians 5:9b-10).

> We will all stand before the judgment seat of God. ... So then each of us will **give an account of himself** to God (Romans 14:10b, 12).

> According to the grace of God given to me, like a skilled master builder I laid a foundation, and someone else is building upon it. Let each one take care how he builds upon it. For no one can lay a foundation other than that which is laid, which is Jesus Christ. Now if anyone **builds on the foundation** with gold, silver, precious stones, wood, hay, straw—each one's work will become manifest, for the day will disclose it, because it will be revealed by fire, and the fire will test what sort of work each one has done. If the work that anyone has built on the foundation survives, **he will receive a reward**. If anyone's work is burned up, **he will suffer loss, though he himself will be saved**, but only as through fire (1 Corinthians 3:10-15).

There are several words or phrases in these verses that are essential to our understanding.[94] First, "judgment seat" is *bēma* (βῆμα), which is a small space (Acts 7:5) or raised

---

[94] These are in bold in the passages to help point back to them.

platform.[95] This platform could be for a public speaker, a judicial bench, or even where the judges watched the games (like the Olympics). When used in a judicial sense, those under examination stood before the *bēma* to receive whatever the judges decided they deserved. This is probably the picture Paul had in mind as he considered Jesus rewarding faithful believers for their work in this life and loss of reward for unfaithfulness. Jesus' judgment will be made as each one gives an account of his or her life and work for the Savior.

The analogy Paul used to describe how Jesus will make his decision is the idea of a building. The fact that Jesus is the foundation reinforces that only believers in Jesus will stand at this judgment. This will not determine a person's salvation or eternal state; only those saved will be there. The question is one of reward for obedience, not salvation for belief. The things we do in this life are compared to "gold, silver, precious stones, wood, hay, straw," some of which are much more valuable than others. As they pass through God's holy fire, only those things of high quality will survive, and these will determine our reward. Loss of reward does not mean loss of salvation. He himself will be saved but without any reward.

This picture of different types of works ties into the phrase "whether good or evil." In this case, it is unfortunate that most translations chose "evil" here. While that is certainly one legitimate understanding, a better translation would be "worthless." Many ancient copies of the passage use the word *phaulos* (φαῦλος) to describe the *quality* of the works rather than

---

[95] Mathew 27:19; John 19:13; Acts 12:21; 18:12, 16, 17; 25:6, 10, 17; Romans 14:10; 2 Corinthians 5:10.

their *morality*. If this was Paul's intention, it matches much better with the picture of "gold, silver, precious stones, wood, hay, straw" in his previous letter to the same church. This helps clarify that, while a person may do many good things in this life, they may not be worthwhile for God's purposes. Our motives and attitudes will be a determining factor in whether our actions are worthy or worthless (1 Corinthians 4:5).

Finally, the word translated "receive what is due" is the Greek verb *komizō* (κομίζω), which occurs only ten times in the New Testament, nine times in the context of repayment or a promise fulfilled.[96] Any rewards (or loss of reward) will be earned or deserved. These are not gifts. These are the fulfillment of God's promise to those who will serve him faithfully, using the spiritual gifts and talents he gave us for his glory and service.

SHOULD WE WORK FOR REWARDS?

As mentioned above, many people are uncomfortable with the idea that God offers rewards for our service. How is that not bribery? The whole concept of Santa Claus (depending on your cultural holiday) is often used by well-meaning adults to coerce children into being good in order to receive presents. Is this what God is relegated to? Is he just a magical being who bribes people into being good?

No, that is not the picture that the Bible presents at all. A better concept than bribery is incentive. What parent does not offer incentives to their children to get them to do certain things?

---

[96] These are Matthew 25:27; 2 Cor 5:10; Ephesians 6:8; Colossians 3:25; Hebrews 10:36; 11:19, 39; 1 Peter 1:9; and 5:4. The tenth, Luke 7:37, simply means "to bring" rather than "to repay."

This is the entire basis of the barter or employment system. One person works for another person, who, in return, gives something to the worker based on the value of the work done.

As seen in chapter two, when a person believes in Jesus for salvation, he or she is immediately adopted into God's family. We are also released from slavery to sin and to Satan, yet God does not require us to immediately become his servants. This is a choice he wants us to make out of love and gratitude toward him. Many believers never choose to dedicate themselves to serving God (*the path* step of excellence), so they will not receive rewards for faithful service. Those who choose to follow *the discipleship path*, spending their time and effort to know Jesus better and love him more—as shown in their service for him—will be rewarded for that.

So, should we care about future rewards? Is it mercenary or ungodly to want rewards for faithful service? Should salvation *not* be enough for us? Of course, we should care about rewards. We have already determined that God came up with the concept of rewards and offered them to us, so it is not wrong to want or work for them. In fact, he encourages us to do so.

> Slaves, obey in everything those who are your earthly masters, not by way of eye-service, as people-pleasers, but with sincerity of heart, fearing the Lord. Whatever you do, work heartily, as for the Lord and not for men, **knowing that from the Lord you will receive the inheritance as your reward**. You are serving the Lord Christ (Colossians 3:22-24).

Even in our daily employment, we are to consider ourselves not working for other people but for the Lord. You are serving the Lord Christ. This attitude is possible because we do know that there is a reward coming, whether we ever gain anything in this life. Just a few verses earlier, Paul described this attitude: "Set your minds on things that are above, not on things that are on earth. For you have died, and your life is hidden with Christ in God" (Colossians 3:23). There is an old saying that someone may be too heavenly-minded to be of earthly good. Paul believed the opposite. He taught that the more heavenly-minded a disciple becomes, the better he or she will be on this earth to those around them. The proper spiritual attitude in a Biblical disciple brings value even to those who do not believe and may even reflect the kindness of God that can lead people to salvation (Romans 2:4).

Thus, while our basis for living rightly should not be getting rewards, God does not think that it is beneath him to incentivize us. God is not ashamed to offer them, so we should not be ashamed to anticipate and desire them. The growing relationship that Biblical disciples have with Jesus in this life will reflect in his kingdom and into eternity. Even further, because the idea of giving rewards was God's, not ours, not wanting one is not humility, it is foolishness. When God tells us to work toward something, how can we say that we should not? "If a reward is a sign of God's approval, we should want that."[97]

> Do you not know that in a race all the runners run, but only one receives the prize? **So, run that you may obtain it**. Every athlete exercises self-control in all things. They do it to receive a perishable wreath, but we an

---

[97] Mark Hitchcock addressing a public session at the Pre-Trib Study Group Conference, Dallas, TX, Dec 12, 2019.

imperishable. So I do not run aimlessly; I do not box as one beating the air. But I discipline my body and keep it under control, lest after preaching to others I myself should be disqualified (1 Corinthians 9:24-27).

WHAT REWARDS DID GOD PROMISE?

For those who are now convinced that God does offer rewards for our faithful service and that it is not sinful to want to receive them, you might have started to wonder what types of rewards God is planning to give. Maybe you have already started to think about what those rewards could be. Before you go too far, consider this story.

> A father tells his son to clean the trash scattered on their property for thirty minutes and he will get a reward. The son does not know what the reward will be but cannot help thinking of the possibilities—money, candy, a new toy—so he eagerly complies. The longer he worked the bigger the reward grew in his mind. What could it be?

> After finishing the full thirty minutes, the son ran toward his dad, excited that the work was done and the reward was at hand. He stood in front of his dad in anticipation. After inspecting the boy's work, the dad finally said, "Your reward is that you and I will throw around a baseball for an hour."[98]

Is that reward better or worse than what the boy anticipated? Would the look in the boy's eyes have darkened when he

---

[98] Feel free to adjust the reward based on your situation—kick a soccer ball, shoot a basketball, etc.

compared what he heard to what he had built up in his mind? Now, what if the dad told his son that they would be throwing the ball at the boy's favorite ballpark? Would that make it better? What if he learned that it would not be just him and his dad alone but that his favorite ballplayer or even his favorite team would be there? At what point does the reward become better than expected? It depends on the boy's expectations and how much information the father did not share at first.

When it comes to future eternal rewards, the Scriptures are mostly silent on what they will be.[99] How much information did the Father withhold while our anticipation grows? The difference between our heavenly Father and the human father in the story is that our heavenly Father can do far beyond whatever we could ask or imagine (Ephesians 3:20). So, when God promised elders a crown for faithful service (1 Peter 5:4) or a person rulership over one or more cities in Jesus' kingdom (Luke 19:11-27), what we may expect compared to the reality of what God knows is vastly different.

> Things that no eye has seen, or ear heard, or mind imagined, are the things God has prepared for those who love him (1 Corinthians 2:9, NET).

While there is much that we do not know, there are some things that we can say with certainty. First, contrary to what many people teach all over the world, God never promised

---

[99] The apostles do speak of four specific crowns but give very little detail about what they include—crown of boasting or rejoicing (1 Thessalonians 2:19), crown of righteousness (2 Timothy 4:8), crown of life (James 1:12), and crown of glory (1 Peter 5:4).

physical health and wealth to believers in this life. Many denominations (often charismatic) make these promises to their followers using only Old Testament promises to Israel as their basis. They cannot use passages from the New Testament—those written to and for the Church—because they do not exist. Surprisingly, the only physical promises that God said Church believers should expect are negative.

> I have said these things to you, that in me you may have peace. In the world you will have tribulation. But take heart; I have overcome the world (John 16:33).

> Indeed, all who desire to live a godly life in Christ Jesus will be persecuted (2 Timothy 3:12).

We are not to worry about the trouble and persecution that will come from those who hate Christ because this life is not our final destination and the Holy Spirit can give us peace in the middle of the chaos, but that does not minimize the fact that we will face it. This is far from the lives of ease and prosperity that many false teachers promise their followers.

Second, we know that any tangible reward that we may receive will come with a personal commendation from God himself.

> So then, do not judge anything before the time. Wait until the Lord comes. He will bring to light the hidden things of darkness and reveal the motives of hearts. Then each will receive recognition from God (1 Corinthians 4:5, NET).

The word translated recognition is *epainos* (ἔπαινος), the normal word for praise in the New Testament. Although we are to spend our lives in praise to God, when we stand before him for judgment and reward, he will praise us. What an amazing thought! Additionally, it seems that God will find something to praise in every believer, not just those who have worked faithfully. Is it possible that his praise will grow with more rewards? Or will he praise every believer while the rewards vary? We cannot know, but we can be sure it will be far more than we can imagine now. Attempting to answer this important question accurately without overstating anything, Geisler put it this way: "Everyone in heaven will be *fully* blessed, but not everyone will be *equally* blessed. Every believer's cup will be full and running over, but not everyone's cup will be the same size. We determine in time what our capacity for appreciating God will be in eternity" (italics original).[100]

Finally, we know that eternity will be a time of service:

No longer will there be anything accursed, but the throne of God and of the Lamb will be in it, and **his servants will worship him**. They will see his face, and his name will be on their foreheads. And night will be no more. They will need no light of lamp or sun, for the Lord God will be their light, and they will reign forever and ever (Revelation 22:3-5).

Will worship, in verse three is often translated, will serve, because it comes from the word *latreuō* (λατρεύω), which means

---

[100] Norman Geisler, *Systematic Theology, Volume Four: Church, Last Things* (Minneapolis, MN: Bethany House Publishers, 2005), 310.

to serve, often about acts of worship. It is the same root word that Paul used in Romans 12:1 for our "reasonable service/worship," depending on your translation. Thus, for eternity we will be worshiping God by serving him. Exactly what this means is uncertain but, based on passages like Luke 19:11-27, we can conclude that there may be levels or ranks of service opportunities available. Faithful service now will prepare us for greater serving responsibilities in Jesus' kingdom and into eternity.

SUMMARY

In this chapter, we have seen that God, in his infinite wisdom, has chosen to offer believers future rewards for faithful lives. While we cannot be sure exactly what these rewards will be, we know that they will be better than anything we could imagine and that God wants us to look forward to them, serving now in anticipation of his praise and commendation later. We also know that these will be awarded to those who intentionally and actively choose to walk *the discipleship path* after dedicating themselves to his service.

I appeal to you therefore, brothers, by the mercies of God, to present your bodies as a living sacrifice, holy and acceptable to God, which is your spiritual worship. Do not be conformed to this world, but be transformed by the renewal of your mind, that by testing you may discern what is the will of God, what is good and acceptable and perfect (Romans 12:1-2).

STUDY QUESTIONS

1. Before reading this chapter, were you aware that God promised future rewards for faithful service? If so, what did you think about this concept? Were you uncomfortable with it?

2. After reading this chapter, are you comfortable with the thought that God wants to reward you? Why or why not?

3. If you were to stand before Jesus right now, do you think your motives would earn you eternal rewards or would you suffer loss? Why?

4. What is the most important truth, principle, or practice you learned from this chapter? What do you plan to do with it?

CHAPTER TEN

WARNINGS FOR THOSE WHO WANDER

The richness and depth of the Letter to the Hebrews – especially about its main subject, Jesus Christ – is unsurpassed. So, of all the topics the writer could have addressed, it may be surprising that he chose to answer one of the questions that the rest of the New Testament writers rarely addressed. Whereas the rest of the New Testament letters encourage believers to stay firm and mature in their faith, and Hebrews does as well, it also dramatically answers another big question: "What if we do not stay firm? What if we walk away? What if we leave *the path*?"

In response, the writer of Hebrews offered five warnings for those who wander. He carefully and methodically proved that there will be a massive, dramatic loss—not a loss of eternal salvation but something else—for believers who choose to not stay on *the path*.

Can a true believer walk away from his or her faith? That by itself is a big question for many people. Many say no, that a true believer will press on. Even if they do wander, it will be for only a short time, but they will come back before they die. They would say that the warnings in Hebrews are either only hypothetical—what might happen to a person if they could fall away—or that the people are only those who have claimed to believe but are not truly saved.[101] There are at least two reasons why neither of these options is legitimate.

First, as much as we wish that were true, that is not the picture given in the New Testament. Paul's repeated appeals for his readers to persevere shows that many of them were not, and the passages we studied in the spiritual growth process outlined in chapter seven above proved that many true believers never grow very far in their faith. Jesus' parable of the four soils (Matthew 13:3-9, 18-23) indicates that a person can spring up quickly in their faith then shrivel away due to external pressure or other internal desires. In his parable, those who shriveled were alive yet never produced a crop for the farmer.

Second, there are three key truths evident in Hebrews that help us understand that the writer had true believers in mind. First, he never questioned his readers' salvation; he always assumed they were believers. He called them brothers and sisters, participants with Christ, etc. Rather than addressing them as unbelievers, he was afraid that they were true believers in danger of walking away from Jesus. Second, it is impossible to walk (or fall) away from something they never

---

[101] Scofield and Morris taught that these people were "close to faith" but had never truly believed. Ryrie said that they were only professing believers (thought they believed but never did), so they could walk away from it.

had. Only a Christian can walk away from Christianity. Third, and most importantly, not once did the writer give a command or encouragement for his readers to believe in Jesus as Savior or Messiah. The only command in the Bible for unbelievers is to believe, which the writer never told them to do. Instead, he encouraged them to not leave what they already had. Could these warnings be useful for counterfeit, professing Christians? Of course; they could certainly lead them to true faith in Christ, but that would be a secondary result, not the writer's main purpose.

> Far from undermining the eternal security of the true believer, this epistle is freighted with many words, expressions, and concepts which affirm this truth in no uncertain terms, as well as to encourage all to personally enter into its full reality. The great irony of the misinterpretations of Hebrews is that this book has more words like confidence/boldness (*parresian* 4t), assurance (*plerophoria* 2t, *hupostaseos* 4t), confirmation (*bebaios* 8t), access (3t), promises (*epangelia* 17t), hope (6t), than any other Bible book. The author not only spoke of Christ's eternal redemption (9:12), eternal salvation (5:9), eternal inheritance (9:15), but furthermore that he saves us forever (7:25), and that we are perfected for all time (10:4). In sum, Christ was sacrificed once-for-all that we might be saved once-for-all (7:25-27; 9:12, 25-6; 10:10-14).[102]

---

[102] C. Gordon Olson, *Beyond Calvinism and Arminianism: An Inductive Mediate Theology of Salvation*, Third Edition: Expanded, Revised, & Updated (Lynchburg, VA: Global Gospel Publishers, 2012), 204.

So, we must answer this question—whether it is possible for a person to wander away from the faith and remain saved—in the positive. While it is certainly not God's plan or intention, yes, it is possible. This is where the Hebrews' warnings come in. So, what happens to that person? If he or she does not lose their eternal salvation, does it matter if they do not persevere in the faith? The five warnings prove that, yes, it matters very much.

There is one more thought about this that we should not overlook. In each of the warnings, the writer used the word we, including himself as one in danger of loss. Certainly, he did not question his own salvation, yet he never said that he was exempt from his teachings. Whoever wrote this letter knew that he could drift and fall away if he did not follow the same principles outlined in this letter.[103] What a sobering concept for each of us.

FOLLOWING THE WRITER'S THOUGHT

How did the writer accomplish his plan of warning his readers of the dangers of falling away? It is not what we might expect. Rather than simply giving warning after warning, listing all the gruesome details of where their lives would end and the disaster they would leave, he couched every warning in the positive doctrinal teaching of the only thing that could preserve them—their relationship with Jesus himself.

---

[103] Although the writer is unknown to us, the original readers knew him well. They had a mutual friend in Timothy (13:23), and the letter shows that he was able to speak with them bluntly as a close friend and teacher. So, it is incorrect to say that the writer was "anonymous"; it is more accurate to say that the original audience did not need him to sign his letter.

The theme of Hebrews is a single core doctrinal truth with an implied warning. In one passage after another, the writer argued that Jesus is better than anyone or anything else we could possibly follow or attach ourselves to.[104] The implied warning, then, is that following anyone or anything else will lead to great personal loss. However, the implied warning was not enough, so the writer gave five specific, graphic warnings for those who would still choose to turn away for any reason. These are found in chapters 2, 3-4, 5-6, 10, and 12. Here is one way to outline the writer's teaching:

Presenting: Jesus the Son (1:1-14)

Warning 1: "Do not neglect and drift away" (2:1-4)

Presenting: Jesus the Man (2:5-3:6)

Warning 2: "Do not harden your heart" (3:7-4:13)

Presenting: Jesus the High Priest, Part 1 (4:14-5:10)

Warning 3: "Do not fall away" (5:11-6:12)

Presenting: Jesus the High Priest, Part 2 (6:13-10:25)

Warning 4: "Do not continue to walk away" (10:26-39)

Exhortation: Faith (11:1-40)

Exhortation: Hope (12:1-13)

Warning 5: "Do not ignore God" (12:14-29)

---

[104] To prove his point, the writer compared Jesus to angels, Moses, Aaron, the entire Levitical priesthood, and the old Mosaic Covenant. Each time he offered several reasons proving Jesus' infinite superiority.

Exhortation: Love (13:1-25)

THE NEED FOR THE WARNINGS

Why were the warnings necessary? Why did the writer see the need to send this to his Jewish friends? In other words, *why do believers walk or fall away from the faith?* There are probably several reasons for this, but here are a few things we should consider.

Based on some of the things the writer included, it seems the original readers were not satisfied with just a spiritual faith. The Judaism which they left when they accepted Jesus as Messiah and Savior was a sensory experience. The altar, blood, incense, etc. were things they could touch, see, and smell. Today, many believers are turning to religions, cults, and practices that embrace ancient rituals—often even pagan things—because they want to see, feel, smell, and taste something in their religion. Believers back then and today think that being able to use their senses would make their faith so much better, but the writer reminds us that it does not work that way. At best, those are simply empty shadows of genuine faith.

Another reason for the warnings was that the original readers were tempted to leave or hide their faith in Jesus because of growing persecution against them (10:33-34; 12:4). The Roman emperor at the time was Nero, who is now infamous for his mental instability and fondness for blaming Jews and Christians for Rome's troubles. This culminated when he watched Rome burn to the ground and set the city against the Christians. Under those circumstances, very few of us would argue with their logic that God would surely forgive them if they hid their faith just until the persecution stopped. This type of thinking continues to be true today as believers are often tempted to be secret Christians so that they will not experience persecution for their faith. Again, the writer warned that they will experience a severe loss if they make that decision.

THE USE OF SALVATION IN HEBREWS

There is one more point to address before examining the five warnings themselves. An often-misunderstood aspect of Hebrews is how the writer used the word salvation. If we miss this, we will completely misunderstand the arguments he made. In the modern Christian context, when people say or read salvation, they usually think only that "Jesus died on the cross for my sins, I'm forgiven, and I'm going to heaven." Born again, or forgiven, equals salvation.[105] For clarity, we will refer to this as eternal salvation.

This is not how the Biblical writers usually thought of salvation, however. In the entire Old Testament Scriptures, only seven percent (60/810) of the uses of *salvation* have to do with eternal salvation. In the New Testament, that number grows to about forty percent (60/150). Statistically, this means that almost ninety percent of the uses of salvation in the Bible refer to something other than eternal salvation.

What, then, does "salvation" mean ninety percent of the time? While the Hebrew verb *yasha`* (יָשַׁע)[106] and the Greek verb

---

[105] Review chapter two for a more complete perspective on the Biblical doctrine of salvation.

[106] This is the root of the name *Yeshua*, the Hebrew name of both Joshua and Jesus, and several others.

sōzō (σῴζω)[107] are often translated "to save," they both have the basic meanings of "to help, deliver, rescue, or preserve; to save from death."[108] Even a cursory search through the Old Testament reveals many times where the writer or speaker asked for salvation in that basic sense of the word. Consider David, for instance, repeatedly crying out, "Save me, O God!" Each time he meant, "Deliver me from my enemies; rescue me from this terrible situation I'm in." Further, nearly every time *yasha* ʿis used with the nation of Israel, it is tied to God's promise to deliver them into Messiah's kingdom. This extended into the New Testament as the Jewish people continued to anticipate the coming kingdom.

Since Hebrews is tied so closely to the Old Testament, we find this basic meaning is the primary use of salvation in Hebrews as well. For instance, in Hebrews 1:14 the writer asked, "Are they not all ministering spirits sent out to serve for the sake of those who are to inherit salvation?" For those who know Jesus as Savior, eternal salvation is something we have right now. It is a gift now, not something that we may or may not inherit later. What could the writer mean? Are there people who will inherit salvation at some point in the future? We must understand Hebrews from the Jewish perspective of the original audience. When they read "those who will inherit salvation," they immediately thought of the coming Messianic kingdom and asked, "What part will I have there?"

---

[107] σῴζω, BDAG, 982.

[108] ישע, Ludwig Koehler et al., *The Hebrew and Aramaic Lexicon of the Old Testament* (Leiden, Netherlands: E.J. Brill, 1996), 448.

This is the full picture of salvation, not just the aspect of eternal salvation—that some believers will reign with the Messiah in his kingdom, that we will serve him in his kingdom, and that we will receive an inheritance in his kingdom. As seen in the previous chapter on eternal rewards, the way we live this life will have a direct impact or correlation to what we will inherit in the kingdom. Eternal salvation is a gift, and all believers will enter the kingdom with Jesus, but many will not find a full inheritance there.

Thus, salvation in Hebrews almost always[109] refers to the inheritance of rewards in the coming kingdom, and the warnings in Hebrews are for all believers who are in danger of falling away from the faith and losing their inheritance in Messiah's kingdom.

FIRST WARNING: "DO NOT NEGLECT AND DRIFT AWAY" (HEBREWS 2:1-4)

In chapter one, the writer presented Jesus as the final revelation from God, making him better and higher than the angels, the prophets, and every other type of revelation before him. For this reason, believers "must pay closer attention to what we have heard" (2:1). What had they heard to this point? They had heard the entire Old Testament, everything God had

---

[109] Hebrew 7:25 is one great example of where salvation does mean forgiveness of sin. Not only is forgiveness the point of the immediate context, it is worth noting that the writer expanded on the verb, stating that Jesus "is able to **save completely** those who come to God through him." He used "save completely" because it was not his normal use of the word "save."

revealed from Genesis to Malachi (the final prophet) and the final and supreme revelation from Jesus himself.

It is precisely because they had heard and knew so much that they were in danger of drifting away. They had grown up hearing the same stories, reading and memorizing the same passages, and singing the same songs over and over so often that they had stopped really hearing them. They had begun to neglect the inherent truth of the Scriptures and were drifting, not just from the Old Testament but from Jesus himself and the truth that he has revealed.

Many people have experienced the uneasy feeling when, after playing for a while in an ocean or lake or river, they discovered that an unseen current had caused them to drift away from where they thought they were and where they intended to be. This was not something they noticed while it happened. It did not take place quickly and was not something they considered to be dangerous. In fact, in most cases, they did not think about it at all until after it was already done.

This life is like a current that never stops moving against God's truth. We are warned that this whole world lies under Satan's power (1 John 5:19; 2 Corinthians 4:4; Ephesians 2:1-3), and the more we attach ourselves to this world, the more we will drift away from the truth of where God wants us to be. Perhaps the greatest cause of drifting from God's truth is a basic, fundamental misunderstanding of it. When we do not understand the truth that God revealed, we are more likely to drift away from it.

The prime example of this is Eve in Genesis 3:1-6. As Adam and Eve stood in the garden God had given to them, the enemy came to them and asked, "Did God really say?"[110] That question set the stage for a misunderstanding of God's revealed truth. He twisted it a little bit, and she twisted it a little more. How can we stay anchored to a truth we do not understand? Further, when we misunderstand what God said and when we misunderstand what God meant, is it any wonder that we find ourselves drifting from it?

> For since the message declared by angels proved to be reliable, and every transgression or disobedience received a just retribution, **how shall we escape if we neglect** such a great salvation? (Hebrews 2:2-3a)

The writer indicated that drifting is a result of neglect. The danger is that we will drift, but the reason that we drift is due to our neglect of the truth. Neglect means to demonstrate a lack of concern or apathy toward something. Believers drift away because of a wrong understanding of revealed truth which leads to a lack of concern for it, and when we have a lack of concern for the truth, where else can we go?

"How shall we escape?" The writer's question is legitimate. When someone broke the Mosaic Law in the Old Testament, they were punished. Breaking the Law came with grave consequences and loss. Sometimes it required an extra sacrifice; sometimes it required death. The penalty may have been different, but there was always punishment. If God's law

---

[110] The text clearly shows that Adam was standing there listening to the entire conversation. In Hebrew, the serpent addressed them with plural verbs ("you both"), and verse six states that she gave the fruit "to her husband who was with her."

was so important that he would punish and kill people for breaking it, how much more important is the revelation given by Jesus himself? Why would believers think we can get away with no consequences for neglecting his truth? Yet how many misuse or abuse verses like 1 John 1:9? Can we sin and simply confess with no consequences or loss? Do we think that the God of grace is so casual about the truth of salvation and inheritance?

If we are going to neither drift nor neglect this truth, we must pay closer attention, not to new revelation but to the old revelation that we already learned. The writer did not say that he had new revelation they needed to learn; he said that they needed to dig back into what they already knew and anchor themselves there. If Biblical disciples do not pay close attention to the truth they already know, they will find themselves drifting away, believing something they never thought they would believe, and living a life so far away from Christ they never thought they would live.

This is the reason it is so important to understand what salvation really is, what Jesus really taught, and what the Scriptures really mean. Sadly, many believers are drifting. We do not question their eternal salvation, just like the writer never questioned the salvation of his readers. They will go to heaven, but they will miss out on so much until then. They will enter the kingdom, but they may have no inheritance there. Each of us is in danger of drifting and neglect if we refuse to pay close attention to what we have been taught.

SECOND WARNING: "DO NOT HARDEN YOUR HEART"

(HEBREWS 3:7-4:13)

The second warning begins at 3:7 and continues almost to the end of chapter four. This passage is a sermon within a sermon. In the first five verses, the writer quoted his text from Psalm 95. The rest of the passage (twenty-one verses) explains and applies that passage for his readers, including us.

In Psalm 95, David referred to a specific event in Israel's history that is essential for understanding this passage. The context is Numbers 13-14. God had miraculously rescued the nation of Israel from Egypt. Over several weeks he led them through the desert to Mount Sinai, where they camped at the foot of the mountain for about a year. During that time, God met with Moses and the Jewish elders multiple times. He gave them his Law, and they entered a special covenant with God, saying, "Everything the Lord has said, we will do!" Of course, they immediately disobeyed by building a golden calf idol and worshiping that instead of God (Exodus 32).

At the end of that year, God said it was time for him to give them the land of Canaan, which he had promised to Abraham, so he led them from Sinai to a point at the southern end of Canaan (now Israel) called Kadesh-Barnea. In Numbers 13, God told Moses to select twelve men, one leader from each of the twelve tribes, to go into the land, gather reconnaissance information, and God would help them conquer the land. When the spies returned forty days later, ten of the twelve said the land was impossible to conquer. The people were too big, the city walls were too strong; they could never win. Only two, Caleb and Joshua, encouraged the people to take God at his word and move forward. The people listened to the other ten and did not go in, bringing God's judgment on them. For forty years (one year for each day the spies were in the land), God had them wander in the desert, like nomads, until that entire generation died, except Caleb and Joshua, who led the new generation into the land.

The failure to trust God at Kadesh-Barnea was such a major event in Israel's history that it became known as *the rebellion*. This was how David referred to it hundreds of years later in Psalm 95, and that was the basis of the second Hebrews warning. Within only thirteen months out of Egypt, their hearts had drifted from God, and they had forgotten all he had done for them since Egypt.

> Therefore, as the Holy Spirit says, Today, if you hear his voice, **do not harden your hearts as in the rebellion**, on the day of testing in the wilderness, where your fathers put me to the test and saw my works for forty years. Therefore, I was provoked with that generation, and said, 'They always go astray in their heart; they have not known my ways.' As I swore in my wrath, '**They shall not enter my rest**.' Take care, brothers, lest there be in any of you an evil, unbelieving heart, leading you to fall away from the living God (Hebrews 3:7-12).

Just as that ancient generation displayed an evil, unbelieving heart and forsook God, the same possibility is true for believers today. Most of the Israelites in the desert were true believers who had shown their faith at Passover before leaving Egypt. In Numbers 14:20, God even forgave them for their rebellion at Kadesh-Barnea, but the physical consequences remained. Even forgiven people suffer consequences for sin. For that first generation of Israelites, the consequence was that they would not enter the land of rest and peace and security that God had promised.

This second warning is the danger of disbelief. When we begin to drift from God and his promises, we may come to a point where we must decide: Will we continue to believe God's promises or turn away from him?

The Greek word translated fall away in verse twelve is *apostēnai* (ἀποστῆναι), a verbal form of the word from which we get apostasy. Apostasy means to fall away, leave, depart. In different contexts, the word can mean full out rebellion, a notice of divorce, or renunciation of a person, group, or doctrine. In Hebrews 11:1, "faith is the assurance of things hoped for." Apostasy in this context, then, is giving up our hope that God can deliver and walking away.

As we discussed above, this is something only a true believer can do. An unbeliever can reject Jesus but cannot fall away from him, so these people must be true believers. The writer never questioned their salvation, only their decision to back away from it. His immediate readers did not think they were turning away from God by going back into Judaism, but they were. Choosing to trust anything else is a rejection of Jesus in that moment and situation.

In the same way that the first warning had a "do this instead," so does the second. "But exhort one another every day, as long as it is called today, that none of you may be hardened by the deceitfulness of sin" (Hebrews 3:13). This is the first of two positive commands for us so that we do not fall away from God. It is every disciple's job to come alongside a fellow believer who seems to be drifting or neglecting and encourage them to not fall away. The deceitfulness of sin is the false conclusion that sin and unbelief do not matter and have no consequences. "The antidote for developing a hard heart is a caring and encouraging community of believers."[111]

There is a reason that the warning passages become increasingly harsher. Watch the pattern of the wandering disciple. Neglect leads to drifting which, in turn, leads to apostasy/falling away, resulting in physical judgment. Because of their unbelief and disobedience, the Israelite people did not enter the land; instead, they died in the desert. Even Moses and Aaron missed it because of their sin, proving that these were not all unbelievers or simply those who professed to believe.

Rest is a keyword in Hebrews which the writer used to refer to both physical and spiritual rest. In this first use, he quoted God who meant physical rest in the land of Canaan. Rest and apostasy do not refer to eternal salvation, which is dependent on God's faithfulness to his promises to us. Future blessings (alternately called salvation/deliverance, rest, and inheritance in Hebrews) are dependent on our belief in his promises and our faithfulness to him. There are spiritual blessings for every believer that cannot be lost (Ephesians 1:3; Colossians 3:1-4), but there are many rewards, inheritances, and blessings that will be based on our faithfulness. Some of these include present ministry opportunities and even physical life itself.

---

[111] Arnold Fruchtenbaum, *The Messianic Jewish Epistles*, (San Antonio, TX: Ariel Ministries, 2004), 48.

"Therefore, while the promise of entering his rest still stands, let us fear lest any of you should seem to have failed to reach it" (Hebrews 4:1). The promise of God's ultimate rest was not voided by the first generation of Israelites or fulfilled by the second. It is still future and open to everyone who would believe. Each generation, each individual believer, needs to decide whether he will live faithfully and enter God's rest or live for himself and not receive present peace and future blessing. The Scriptures are clear that there is a point of no return when rebellion is made permanent, often resulting in physical death. This was true for the ancient generation at Kadesh-Barnea; it was true for the readers of Hebrews in AD 70 when Rome destroyed Jerusalem; and it remains true for believers today. The choice must be made *today*.

> For the word of God is living and active, sharper than any two-edged sword, piercing to the division of soul and of spirit, of joints and of marrow, and discerning the thoughts and intentions of the heart. And no creature is hidden from his sight, but all are naked and exposed to the eyes of him to whom we must give account (Hebrews 4:12-13).

God examines our lives with his Word. This is true now (James 1:22-25) but also in the future at the Bema, when he will "dissect" our works to reveal how faithful we were and reward us (2 Corinthians 5:10). The living God produced a living Word that has the power to change us now, but he will also use it to evaluate us later. No believer can escape God's evaluation.

THIRD WARNING: "DO NOT FALL AWAY"

(HEBREWS 5:11-6:12)

This is the best known of the five warnings and may be the second-best known section of Hebrews, second only to the list of names in chapter eleven. This passage is also widely debated, and it requires careful attention to handle it correctly. While the warning itself is in Hebrews 6:4-8, the last paragraph of chapter five (5:11-14) sets the tone for the entire section, proving that the theme is about disciples growing in their faith, not eternal salvation.

> About this we have much to say, and it is hard to explain, since you have become dull of hearing. For though by this time you ought to be teachers, you need someone to teach you again the basic principles of the oracles of God. You need milk, not solid food, for everyone who lives on milk is unskilled in the word of righteousness, since he is a child. But solid food is for the mature, for those who have their powers of discernment trained by constant practice to distinguish good from evil (Hebrews 5:11-14).

The writer began with the understanding that his readers had at one time made progress in their spiritual lives, but they had since become dull of hearing. They had stopped listening to and practicing the truth; they had started drifting. Because of this, they had gone back to needing milk, not solid food. Although they had been believers long enough that some or all of them should have been able to be teachers by this time, instead they needed someone to teach [them] the basic principles again.

This reminds us of at least three important points about spiritual maturity. First, it is a process. As we saw in chapter seven, there are babies and adults and everything in between. Second, spiritual maturity is God's plan and expectation. Maturity is not simply a suggestion; God expects us to grow. A believer who does not grow spiritually is as unhealthy as a baby who does not develop physically or mentally. Third, spiritual maturity takes training and practice. The spiritual life is not stagnant. Believers who are not intentionally becoming more mature will, by default, become less mature. There is only forward progress or backward drifting. The spiritual life does not stand still.

> Therefore, let us leave the elementary doctrine of Christ and go on to maturity, not laying again a foundation of repentance from dead works and of faith toward God, and of instruction about washings, the laying on of hands, the resurrection of the dead, and eternal judgment. And this we will do if God permits (Hebrews 6:1-3).

Therefore continues the preceding paragraph and provides the call to action due to the state of immaturity the writer found in his readers— let us...go on to maturity. A person cannot saunter or stroll into maturity; he must intentionally move there, as 5:11-14 showed. Because of the nature of spiritual growth, the writer had to encourage his readers, who had been slipping, to move forward in their growth, so he listed a few teachings that he considered to be beginner-level information upon which he expected the spiritual maturity of his readers would build. Because these were all foundational teachings in both Judaism and Christianity (albeit with different applications), he used this opportunity to encourage his readers to move on in their maturity. It's time to grow up, and the writer of Hebrews is helping us to do that.

> For it is impossible, in the case of those who have once been enlightened, who have tasted the heavenly gift, and have shared in the Holy Spirit, and have tasted the goodness of the word of God and the powers of the age to come, and then have fallen away, to restore them again to repentance, since they are crucifying once again the Son of God to their own harm and holding him up to contempt (Hebrews 6:4-6).

For is an explanatory word. In this case, it is how the writer proceeded to explain *why* deliberate spiritual maturity and growth were not to be considered optional and why the readers needed to move beyond their elementary teachings.

"Enlightened...tasted...shared...tasted...and then have fallen away"– many have tried to make the case that these words describe someone close to salvation but not a true believer. However, when taken together, and especially when understood in the broader context of Hebrews, we find a different story altogether. Here is how the writer used these same words elsewhere in his letter:

- There was a specific point in these believers' past when they were enlightened, marking the distinction between their unbelief and belief in Jesus as Messiah (10:32).

- Jesus "experienced death on behalf of everyone" (2:9). He did not have just a little taste. He went through it fully, came out the other side, and was changed because of it.

- These very same readers were "partners in a heavenly calling" (3:1) and had "become partners with Christ" (3:14) through their eternal salvation.

The writer used these same words to describe believers throughout his letter. It is incomprehensible that he would use identical language for two completely different groups of people. The people described in this passage are unquestionably believers.

In the first warning, the writer warned his Christian readers about drifting away from the truth through negligence. Secondly, he warned them about having an unbelieving heart and failing to keep trusting God. He now referred to the same apostasy in a third way.

The word translated, having fallen away, is *parapiptō* (παραπίπτω, to fall by the wayside) and is not the same word found in chapter three. This word does not occur anywhere else in the New Testament, indicating that it is not an experience or state that is normal for a believer; it is an aberration, an anomaly, yet still a possibility.

For someone who does truly fall away from their faith, it is impossible...to restore [him] again to repentance. This signifies that the writer was no longer talking about just drifting. This falling away is the hardening of the unbelieving heart from the second warning. According to the writer, a believer can backslide or walk so far from God that he or she reaches a point of unbelief from which they can no longer repent and return to their previous state of maturity. In the case of the original audience of Hebrews, the point of no return was probably finalized with their physical deaths during the destruction of Jerusalem and the Temple in AD 70, just a few years later.

This is a difficult teaching for many people to accept, and it would be easy to dismiss or reinterpret it if this were the only place we found this concept, but it is not. Jesus, James, Paul, and John also spoke about a point of no return for believers who leave the faith (John 15:1-6; James 5:19-20; 1 Corinthians 11:27-32; 1 John 5:16-17). In each of these passages, we find a believer who fails at some point in his spiritual maturity. Though the call is made to repent, in each case, they refuse to heed the call and find a point of no return resulting in physical death.

It is important to remember that this is not a renewal to forgiveness or eternal salvation that is at stake here. Eternal salvation was secured when they believed in Jesus and does not need to be done again. The entire context of Hebrews 5 and 6 is the maturity of believers, not the salvation of unbelievers. The description is of a believer who falls off *the path* toward spiritual maturity, regressing to the status of an infant in need of milk but refusing even that. It is this person—who knows better, who has seen the goodness available through a growing relationship with Christ—who chooses to throw it away for his own physical safety and his own plan. This person is "not fit" to be associated with Jesus (Luke 9:57-62). He is to be removed from fellowship with the church (Matthew 18:15-17) and turned back out into Satan's world where he thinks he wants to be (1 Corinthians 5:1-5; 1 Timothy 1:18-20).

For land that has drunk the rain that often falls on it and produces a crop useful to those for whose sake it is cultivated, receives a blessing from God. But if it bears thorns and thistles, it is worthless and near to being cursed, and its end is to be burned (Hebrews 6:7-8).

Many have pushed hard against this truth that there is a point of no return. They argue, "Where is the grace, the love, the forgiveness? Is God so harsh that he would not allow them back? What if they didn't know what they were doing?" Knowing how hard of a truth this was for his readers (then and now!) to accept, the writer explained it in another way.

He was clear that this falling away was not a momentary lapse of judgment. This is not, "I messed up, but God refuses to let me come back." Not only has this believer "tasted the goodness of the word of God and the powers of the age to come" (verse five), he also has had the rain of God's Word and blessing and power frequently falling on him. This disciple was once on the road to maturity, but he began to wander. Further and further he spiraled downward— drifting, neglecting, hardening his heart, not accepting the Father's loving discipline (12:5-13)— until he passed the point of a spiritual infant (where some of the immediate readers had already fallen, 5:11-14). Falling away is a road marked by spiritual apathy resulting in the rejection of the Savior. Paul wrote that this type of person "is warped and sinful; he is self-condemned" (Titus 3:11). This is not a one-time decision or instantaneous development that the person will regret the next morning. It is a conscious willful walking away from what he knows to be true.

On the other hand, growing, maturing believers will take God's blessings and turn them into "a crop useful" —great acts of worship and fruitful service for their Lord. Thorns and thistles come from a believer's heart that is not devoted to God. This was the cause of God's ancient lament, "These people say they are mine. They honor me with their lips, but their hearts are far from me" (Isaiah 29:13, NLT). It is the message of many of Jesus' teachings, the New Testament apostles' exhortations, and the Old Testament prophets' warnings.

Whereas the person who receives God's blessings (and sometimes the necessary discipline) provides useful vegetation, the one who continues in his rejection of Christ becomes useless. In 1 Corinthians 9:27 Paul used the same word (*adokimos*, ἀδόκιμος) to say that, if he did not continue serving faithfully, he would be disqualified. Nothing could make us believe that Paul was in fear for his eternal salvation. He was afraid that he would lose the privilege of preaching the gospel he so loved. Paul did not want to be disqualified or rejected from service in this life.

Contrary to how many people interpret this passage, the result of this falling away is not that the person is cursed. We might be able to understand that as a loss of eternal salvation. The writer specifically claimed that the person would be near to being cursed. We could say he is as far from God and as close to being cursed as a true believer could ever be.

Again, the concept of burning leads people to think this means that the believer will go to hell, but neither the context nor the rest of the New Testament teaches this. The analogy is about the treatment of a piece of land, not a person. When a piece of land grows only thorns and weeds, no matter how the owner tries to rejuvenate it, sometimes the only solution is to burn it.

This often results in the land being unable to grow anything again, but it does not change the fact that it is still earth.[112] In the same way, the eternal state of the person remains unchanged; he or she is eternally saved. However, much like a burnt parcel of ground, the person will never again have the opportunity to produce anything useful for its owner. As seen in the Corinthian believers abusing the Lord's table and other passages shown above, this form of divine discipline may be premature physical death. The idea is further developed and applied to all believers in 1 Corinthians 3:10-15, where our works will be judged by God's holy fire at the judgment seat of Christ. The worthless results will be burnt up, though the person himself will be saved, even if he has nothing to show for his life and no inheritance in the kingdom.

In contrast to the common understanding that this passage teaches the loss of eternal salvation as the result of an unknown or arbitrary definition of falling away, we find a God who pursues his people, encouraging a growing relationship with him. However, if someone knowingly, willingly runs away, there is a point at which nothing in heaven or on earth could cause him to be restored to the status he once enjoyed with God. The result is a life of misery, possibly a premature physical death, and a complete loss of reward in eternity. Yet even with all that, God will not curse him forever, because there is "no condemnation for those who are in Christ Jesus" (Romans 8:1),

---

[112] While it is possible that the ground could recover and grow crops again, we would compare that to God's severe discipline on a sinning believer. This passage is referring to someone who never responds positively to that repeated conviction and discipline and so becomes completely scorched and useless forever.

who have been "sealed for the day of redemption" (Ephesians 4:30; 1:13-14).

The application for the ancient readers is the same for us today: there is no such thing as a Christian on hold. We are either growing in our relationship with God or falling away from him. Should we leave our relationship unchecked, maturity can become immaturity, then apathy, and finally outright rejection.

FOURTH WARNING: "DO NOT CONTINUE TO WALK AWAY" (HEBREWS 10:26-39)

This is the most difficult of the five warnings in Hebrews. Because it does not hold back in its graphic description of the potential punishment, many people have come to question their eternal salvation or the eternal salvation of others, especially those they love. The passage is comprised of two important parts—the actual warning (Hebrews 10:26-31) followed by an encouragement to persevere (10:32-39)—but the second part is often ignored.

> For if we go on sinning deliberately after receiving the knowledge of the truth, there no longer remains a sacrifice for sins, but a fearful expectation of judgment, and a fury of fire that will consume the adversaries (Hebrews 10:26-27).

If believers choose to deliberately keep on sinning after receiving the knowledge of the truth, we prove that we have rejected that truth. What is the truth? It is everything the Scriptures (especially Hebrews) have taught us about who Jesus is, what he did, and what he is doing right now as our high priest. It is not a coincidence that the writer's teaching on Jesus is complete at this point. In the final three chapters, he focused on the triad of faith, hope, and love. Chapter eleven shows people who lived in faith. Chapter twelve addresses our final hope, even in the last warning. Chapter thirteen offers practical examples of what God's love looks like when Biblical disciples live it out well.

The whole letter has been about not turning away from Jesus, not holding fast to our faith, not persevering in our obedience. Specifically, the writer gave three commands at the end of the previous section: 1) draw near to God with full faith; 2) hold unwaveringly to the hope that we confess; and 3) spur one another on to love and good works (10:22-24). This is the deliberate sin with which the writer was concerned. If we turn away from God, from our confession, and from our church family, there is nowhere to go except back into Satan's world, and in doing so we have essentially sided with those who crucified Jesus and agreed that they were right. What can God do except judge us? It is this reason that people conclude that believers can lose their eternal salvation, but the passage is more than just those two verses.

> Anyone who has set aside the Law of Moses dies without mercy on the evidence of two or three witnesses. How much worse punishment, do you think, will be deserved by the one who has spurned the Son of God, and has profaned the blood of the covenant by which he was sanctified, and has outraged the Spirit of grace? (Hebrews 10:28-29).

The judgment for completely rejecting the law of Moses was physical death, regardless of the person's spiritual condition. In fact, under the law, there was no sacrifice available for willful, deliberate sin (Numbers 15:30-31). Death was the only option. Notice who is judged, however. This is a person who has been sanctified. This verb—to set apart, sanctify, make holy—*hagiazō*, ἁγιάζω) is used several times in the New Testament, including in Hebrews, to refer to a person's right spiritual condition before God.[113]

Paul told the Romans that "there is no condemnation for those who are in Christ Jesus" (Romans 8:1). Too often, Christians have this idea that no condemnation means no punishment, as if the two were the same. They are not. A believer cannot be eternally condemned because he or she has been joined with Christ. We will, however, all certainly be judged by him expressly because we are joined with him.

To simplify it, every person will one day stand before God and be judged on two issues: our response in faith to God's revelation (eternal salvation) and our living out of God's law (sanctification, maturity, faithfulness).[114] The first determines our eternal state—condemned or justified, separated from God or with him forever. The second determines our eternal status—rewards or punishment and loss.

---

[113] Acts 20:32; 26:18; 1 Corinthians 1:2; 6:11; 1 Thessalonians 5:23; Hebrews 2:11; 9:13-14; 10:10, 14.

[114] There are those who say that a Christian is not under any law at all, but this is not true. We are not bound to the Mosaic Law of the Old Testament, but we are still under God's perfect standard. Every command in the New Testament shows that there is a law which God expects us to obey. We could call it "the law of Christ" (Galatians 6:2).

For we know him who said, "Vengeance is mine; I will repay." And again, "The Lord will judge his people. It is a fearful thing to fall into the hands of the living God" (Hebrews 10:30-31).

These are quotes from Deuteronomy 32:35-36, where God promised to destroy the pagan nations because of their idolatry but restore Israel, even though they had worshiped other gods. Notice, the Lord will judge *his* people. These were God's people in Deuteronomy, and the writer applied it to the believers in Hebrews as well. We must not think we can do anything we want without consequence or punishment, simply because we are God's people. Israel did not get away with it, and neither can Biblical disciples.[115]

When considering whether it is worth turning away, even a little bit, the question we must weigh is this: Is it better to fall under the judgment of the unbelievers around us in this life or under the judgment of God in the next? That was the warning—do not choose to walk away from him or we will suffer judgment for it. Fortunately, each warning comes with an encouragement, how to stay strong and persevere. Lest we think the original readers were only being immature because things became a little inconvenient for them, the writer shares the bigger picture.

But recall the former days when, after you were enlightened, you endured a hard struggle with sufferings,

---

[115] This contradicts the theory that every reference for believers to fear the Lord means only to respect him. It is true that we have no reason to fear him unless we are standing against him, but this is what deliberate sin is. We should fear the punishment that we earn. This is no different than any relationship between a child and a good father.

sometimes being publicly exposed to reproach and affliction, and sometimes being partners with those so treated. For you had compassion on those in prison, and you joyfully accepted the plundering of your property, since you knew that you yourselves had a better possession and an abiding one (Hebrews 10:32-34).

Their connection to the Christian faith was affecting their daily lives, and at least some of them (enough for this writer to address it) thought that it would be much better to leave the Christian group and return to their old friends and religion. They thought they were willing to trade in their better possession for temporary, earthly possessions and relationships. They were honestly questioning if Christianity was worth what it was costing them, but in doing so they forgot what it really cost—the death of Christ.

This is comparable to Jesus' rebuke of the believers in Ephesus in Revelation 2:1-7. They had the correct doctrine and were doing the correct things, but they had left their first love. They had traded a relationship for religion, so Jesus told them, "Remember therefore from where you have fallen; repent and do the works you did at first. If not, I will come to you and remove your lampstand from its place, unless you repent" (Revelation 2:5).

Both the writer of Hebrews and Jesus said to remember what their relationship used to be like. There was joy and hope, something they had lost. If they did not return to him, there would be physical consequences. For the Ephesians, they died, and their church never recovered; Jesus put out their light.

Therefore, do not throw away your confidence, which has a great reward. For you have need of endurance, so that when you have done the will of God you may receive what is promised (Hebrews 10:35-36).

Before listing some of their favorite heroes of the past, pointing to their faithfulness in chapter eleven, the writer said, "Look at your own past faithfulness. It's not only your heroes who have done this well. Don't throw away what you started!"

Falling away, choosing to turn away from Jesus, deliberately sinning in this way is called throwing away one's confidence. It is basically saying, "I won't trust God anymore." Choosing to persevere, however, comes with a great reward. We do not need endurance to receive eternal salvation; that is a gift. We do need endurance to receive the promised rewards.

For Yet a little while, and the coming one will come and will not delay; but my righteous one shall live by faith, and if he shrinks back, my soul has no pleasure in him. But we are not of those who shrink back and are destroyed, but of those who have faith and preserve their souls (Hebrews 10:37-39).

The writer includes a series of quotations from Isaiah and Habakkuk to remind us that Jesus will return as promised, on time, and that those who remain faithful will be rewarded, while the unfaithful will face God's disappointment rather than a "Well done!"

There is still a question about verse thirty-nine—some may "shrink back and are destroyed." How we define two words will determine how we understand this verse. In the New

Testament, the word translated destroyed (*apōleia*, ἀπώλεια) can mean eternal destruction or something wasted (like the perfume used on Jesus' feet, Matthew 26:8) and other things in between. In the Old Testament (which is the main context of Hebrews) it usually refers to physical death.

The word translated souls (*psuchē*, ψυχῆ) also has a range of meanings that includes both eternal soul and physical life. Thus, this sentence can mean shrink back to eternal destruction...have faith and preserve their souls. It can also legitimately mean shrink back and die as a waste...have faith and preserve their lives. Based on the entire context of Hebrews and the vast support of the New Testament which focuses on physical life and future rewards, the second interpretation seems to be better. Thus, the underlying question they needed to answer, and we do as well, is: can we, will we, find total sufficiency in Christ alone or will we waste our lives and lose everything he designed us for?

FIFTH WARNING: "DO NOT IGNORE GOD"

(HEBREWS 12:14-29)

This warning is essentially the writer's final effort to convince his readers that they should rethink their plans to turn away from their Christian faith.

> Strive for peace with everyone, and for the holiness without which no one will see the Lord. See to it that no one fails to obtain the grace of God; that no root of bitterness springs up and causes trouble, and by it many become defiled; that no one is sexually immoral or unholy like Esau, who sold his birthright for a single meal (Hebrews 12:14-16).

The wording here is interesting. *Strive for peace* and *see to it* are both plural; these are commands for the local church community. We are to watch out for each other. However, the three *no ones* are all singular. The church community is tasked with making sure that no individual wanders off *the path* in any of these ways. This cannot happen on Sunday mornings; it requires personal relationships, knowing each other. It is not just about studying the Bible, although that is important; it is about being able to share our lives in such a way that our stories help others and theirs help us. When that does not happen well, even one person wandering off *the path* can cause many [to] become defiled because they become a deep root of bitterness within the church community.

> For you know that afterward, when [Esau] desired to inherit the blessing, he was rejected, for he found no chance to repent, though he sought it with tears (Hebrews 12:17).

Although Esau did not know anything about Jesus, he is still an example of a believer turning away from Jesus. He was promised a blessing if he remained faithful, but he rejected it. Because he turned his back and did not repent, he was rejected.

This translation of "found no chance to repent" is not the best. It almost sounds like it was not Esau's fault. "I tried but I didn't have the opportunity." That was not the situation at all. The NASB and KJV are better—"he found no place for repentance." There was no place in his heart for repentance; he was not interested in repentance, even though he had plenty of opportunities.

The word rejected (*apodokimazō*, ἀποδοκιμάζω) is similar to the concept of disqualified in the previous warnings. It refers to something that has been carefully evaluated, determined to be worthless, and rejected. Based on Esau's actions of disloyalty to God and his promises, Esau was rejected as worthless in reference to God's blessings, and the writer of Hebrews warned believers not to make the same mistake. The blessings and inheritance promised to Esau were legitimately his, but he threw them away by his actions. Just because God made a general promise, it does not necessarily follow that everyone will receive it.

> See that you do not refuse him who is speaking. For if they did not escape when they refused him who warned them on earth, much less will we escape if we reject him who warns from heaven. At that time his voice shook the earth, but now he has promised, Yet once more I will shake not only the earth but also the heavens (Hebrews 12:25-26).

After a few illustrations from the Old Testament to encourage his readers to persevere, the writer finally arrived at the actual warning. Make sure you are not one who follows the example of those who disobeyed before. How could he have made this stronger? Moses talked directly with God and received God's Law, written by God's own finger, and they still rejected it. How could we do any worse? We can do that by rejecting God himself, speaking to us in the person of the eternal Son, Jesus. Those who reject the message of the apostles and the New Testament are not rejecting a great prophet like Moses; they are rejecting the very Word of God Incarnate. How can someone think they could escape the consequences of such unfaithfulness? The Israelites suffered the earthly consequence—death—because of their rebellion, but believers will suffer an eternal consequence in loss of relationship with God and blessing in this life and relationship and inheritance in the next if we turn away and do not repent.

> This phrase, Yet once more, indicates the removal of things that are shaken—that is, things that have been made—in order that the things that cannot be shaken may remain. Therefore, let us be grateful for receiving a kingdom that cannot be shaken, and thus let us offer to God acceptable worship, with reverence and awe, for our God is a consuming fire (Hebrews 12:27-29).

The fact that all believers are fellow heirs with Jesus and will receive a part in his eternal kingdom is never questioned. Even God's judgment could never take that away because there is no condemnation for those who are in Christ Jesus. Because of our eternal relationship with God through Christ, let us offer to God acceptable worship so that we bring him glory and do not lose out on our future inheritance.

SUMMARY

Whereas the entire New Testament encourages believers to commit to spiritual growth, only Hebrews goes into detail to explain what happens for those who choose to not make this commitment. The writer explained that forgetting the true person and work of Christ which brought eternal salvation—demonstrated by an unwillingness to commit to him—can lead to spiritual drifting, then neglect, and ultimately turning away from God altogether. If the believer continues walking away—intentionally, willfully, deliberately—he or she could reach a point of no return where repentance is impossible and physical death may be the result.

The only solution is to pay attention to the truth of Christ presented in Scripture. We should be actively walking *the path*, gradually learning to know him better and love him more, and we should be working to help our fellow believers do the same. This will build up both the individual believers and the church community as we store up for ourselves inheritance and rewards in Jesus' kingdom and into eternity.

STUDY QUESTIONS

1. Have you seen the process of falling away taking place in your life or someone else's? What was required to bring that person back to Jesus, if they came back?

2. Based on the truths discussed in this chapter, do you think you are better equipped to help someone avoid the dangers of wandering and stay on *the path*?

3. Is there anything you are hanging onto in this life—something you think is worth more than your relationship with Jesus—that could be costing you everything of true value both now and in eternity?

4. What is the most important truth, principle, or practice you learned from this chapter? What do you plan to do with it?

CHAPTER ELEVEN

A BRIEF EXAMINATION OF FUTURE EVENTS

Why should we include a chapter on the end times in a book about salvation and discipleship? The reason is that everything we do in this life sets us up for the next. Believing or rejecting Jesus determines our destiny, and believers' obedience or wandering determines eternal rewards. Knowing what is still to come should motivate us for evangelism and ministry now. Specifically, knowing these things helps answer three questions appropriate to close our study:

1) What happens to those who never believe in Jesus?
2) What happens to those who believe in Jesus but never grow spiritually?
3) What happens to those who believe in Jesus and make the effort to mature?

Eschatology is the theological term meaning study of the end times. It covers only those things prophesied in the Bible that have not yet taken place. Much has been written and taught on this doctrine, and it is beyond the scope of this chapter to offer more than a summary. For a much more detailed study, I highly recommend *Understanding End Times Prophecy* (Benware) and *Things to Come* (Pentecost).[116]

The timeline of events presented here follows the same traditional dispensational perspective and literal interpretation of the Bible as those two books.[117] It is offered with the understanding that we can interpret prophecy only so far as God has revealed the details to us. The way we understand the events which God has prophesied throughout the Scriptures does not limit his power or creativity in bringing about the actual details of those events. Thus, this list is complete only as God has allowed us to understand in part what he knows in full.

The succinct version is that God will send a series of judgments on this world to prove his identity and deity and to demonstrate unbelieving humanity's willful rebellion against him. This will be followed by Jesus' visible and physical return to earth to execute his enemies and establish his long-awaited kingdom. After one thousand years, he will stop one last attempt to overthrow him, perform the final judgment on all unbelievers, and all creation will move into eternity. The rest of this chapter will provide more details on each of these events.

---

[116] Paul N. Benware, *Understanding End Times Prophecy: A Comprehensive Approach, Revised and Expanded* (Moody Publishers, 2006); J. Dwight Pentecost, *Things to Come: A Study in Biblical Eschatology* (Zondervan Publishing House, 1958).

[117] For more information on traditional dispensationalism based on the literal interpretation of the Bible, see *What is Dispensationalism?* (Wynnewood, OK: Grace Abroad Ministries, 2018) and Charles C. Ryrie, *Dispensationalism* (Chicago, IL: Moody Publishers, 2007).

RAPTURE

The rapture of the church should be one of the most precious prophecies and doctrines for believers. Although the English word rapture does not occur in the New Testament, it is from the Latin translation of the Greek verb *harpazō* (ἁρπάζω) in 1 Thessalonians 4:13-18. The word means to seize or snatch or take away by force and refers to the event when Jesus will take all believers since the beginning of the church in AD 33 to be with him. Those who have died will be resurrected; the rest will be snatched away and will receive new bodies no longer cursed by sin.

> For the Lord himself will descend from heaven with a cry of command, with the voice of an archangel, and with the sound of the trumpet of God. And the dead in Christ will rise first. Then we who are alive, who are left, will be caught up together with them in the clouds to meet the Lord in the air, and so we will always be with the Lord (1 Thessalonians 4:16-17).

> Behold! I tell you a mystery. We shall not all sleep, but we shall all be changed, in a moment, in the twinkling of an eye, at the last trumpet. For the trumpet will sound, and the dead will be raised imperishable, and we shall be changed (1 Corinthians 15:51-52).

There are at least two purposes for the rapture. First, Jesus wants believers to be with him. Just hours before he was arrested and crucified, Jesus gave the bewildered apostles this encouragement:

Let not your hearts be troubled. Believe in God; believe also in me. In my Father's house are many rooms. If it were not so, would I have told you that I go to prepare a place for you? And if I go and prepare a place for you, I will come again and will take you to myself, that where I am you may be also (John 14:1-3).

His goal has never been to simply leave us here. "I will not leave you as orphans; I will come to you" (John 14:18). From the beginning of creation, God's desire has always been to be present in a close relationship with humanity. Each year at the Christmas season we are reminded that one of Jesus' titles is "Immanuel,"[118] a Hebrew phrase meaning "God with us" (Isaiah 7:14; Matthew 1:23). Sin has made it so that it is not possible at this time, but God's overarching plan has always been moving toward that goal.[119]

A second purpose of the rapture is to rescue the church from the judgments that God will pour out onto this world. Since God's wrath is not directed toward believers, he will take us away first, and he will supernaturally protect anyone who comes to believe during the judgments. "God has not destined us for wrath, but to obtain salvation through our Lord Jesus Christ" (1 Thessalonians 5:9). At the end of both of Paul's passages on the rapture in 1 Thessalonians, he urged that this doctrine should be an encouragement to believers. "Therefore encourage one

---

[118] This word is often spelled with either an initial "I" or "E," and both are correct. *Immanuel* is the Hebrew phrase in Isaiah; *Emmanuel* is the Greek transliteration used in Matthew.

[119] See "A Final Thought" at the end of this book for a brief survey of Bible passages showing God's desire to be present with His people.

another with these words" (1 Thessalonians 4:18). "Therefore encourage one another and build one another up, just as you are doing" (1 Thessalonians 5:11).

BEMA

Following the rapture, everyone who has believed in Jesus since his resurrection will stand before him to give an account of how they served him since they believed. This is called the *Bema* or the judgment seat of Christ. Chapter nine gives a detailed explanation of this judgment. Each believer will be rewarded based on the level of growth and maturity they achieved in this life and for the ministry they accomplished for Jesus. Works of good quality will earn eternal rewards; works of poor quality will count for nothing.

TRIBULATION

After Jesus has removed the church from earth, there will be seven years during which both God and Satan will wreak havoc and destruction on this planet. Jesus said that this time will be so devastating that "if those days had not been cut short, no human being would" survive (Matthew 24:22). The reason for this is because "there will be great tribulation, such as has not been from the beginning of the world until now, no, and never will be" (Matthew 24:21).

Although this period is often called the tribulation, that term is never used for the entire time. Jesus said that the second half of that time will contain great tribulation, but there are two more accurate names for this period. The first is found in Jeremiah 30:7 and translated variously as "the time of Jacob's trouble" (KJV), "the time of Jacob's distress" (NASB), the time of distress for Jacob" (ESV), and "the time of trouble for the descendants of Jacob" (NET). All these show that the central character of this act on the world stage will be Israel. After thousands of years of waiting for their Messiah to come, this period of judgment will finally bring them to the point where they will believe that Jesus is their Messiah.

> "In the whole land," declares the LORD, "two thirds shall be cut off and perish, and one third shall be left alive. And I will put this third into the fire, and refine them as one refines silver, and test them as gold is tested. They will call upon my name, and I will answer them." I will say, 'They are my people;'" and they will say, "The LORD is my God" (Zechariah 13:8-9).

The second name for this time is Daniel's seventieth week. This comes from Daniel 9:24-27 in which Daniel prophesied a series of events for the nation of Israel over 490 years in seven-year increments. The first 483 years ended when Jesus was crucified, but the final seven years did not begin immediately. According to Daniel 9:27, a coming world ruler will make a seven-year peace treaty with Israel that he will break halfway through. It seems that, as part of the covenant, this ruler would build a temple in Jerusalem (or help have it built) so that the Jewish people could resume their animal sacrifices. The apostle John called this coming ruler the antichrist (1 John 2:18), and Paul described him as a man who "opposes and exalts himself against every so-called god or object of worship, so that he takes his seat in the temple of God, proclaiming himself to be God" (2 Thessalonians 2:4).

Called *the beast* in the book of Revelation, he will attempt to destroy Israel and anyone who has come to believe in Jesus

(Revelation 12:17). Over his global empire he will establish the infamous *mark of the beast*, a requirement for anyone who will attempt to buy or sell under his reign (Revelation 13:16-18). The antichrist will be possessed or empowered by Satan himself, which is where he will gain the miraculous power to accomplish all these things (2 Thessalonians 2:9-10; Revelation 13:1-8). During the second forty-two months, God will supernaturally protect Jews and believers.

SECOND COMING

Knowing that he could never defeat God directly, Satan believes he has found a loophole in God's prophetic plan. Before his death and resurrection, Jesus declared to the Jewish people, "I tell you, you will not see me again, until you say, 'Blessed is he who comes in the name of the Lord'" (Matthew 23:39). For the past two thousand years, Satan has made unending attempts to eradicate the Jewish people from existence. If he could annihilate Israel, they could not turn back to Jesus, and Jesus could not return to earth and fulfill prophecy, including defeating Satan. So, in a final effort to destroy Israel, Antichrist will attack Jerusalem. At this point Jesus will finally return to earth and destroy Antichrist and his army (Revelation 19:19-21; Isaiah 63:1-3), sending him and his false prophet to the lake of fire for eternity.

Bible teachers often confuse the second coming with the rapture and teach that the church must be present during the tribulation judgments, but there are many differences that help us understand that they are two separate events for two groups at two times. Here are a few of the differences. In the rapture, Jesus will come *for* the church. In the second coming, he will return *with* the church. In the rapture, he will come only into the clouds. In the second coming, he will return to earth. In the rapture, believers will go with him to heaven. In the second coming, believers will enter the kingdom. A purpose of the rapture is to escape God's wrath, while the second coming is to conclude God's wrath.

JUDGMENTS

After Jesus rescues Jerusalem and the Jewish people from the destruction intended by the antichrist, he will oversee a series of judgments to prepare humanity for his kingdom. One judgment will be on the nation of Israel only. In Ezekiel 20:33-38, God told Israel that he would enter into judgment with them, purifying those who believe and removing all rebels, so that the nation would stand in perfect covenant when the kingdom commences.

A second judgment will be for all the surviving gentiles in the world. This is detailed in Matthew 25:31-46. Although it is frequently misapplied to the church today, this passage shows the fulfillment of one part of the covenant that God made with Abraham and extended to the entire nation of Israel. In Genesis 12:3, God told Abraham, "I will bless those who bless you, and him who dishonors you I will curse." While this has certainly taken place throughout world history, nowhere will it be more evident than at the sheep and goat judgment. According to Matthew, all gentiles who survived the seventieth week will stand before the King and be judged on how they treated the Jewish people— "the least of these my brothers." Those who helped the Jews or treated them well (clothed them, fed them, visited them in prison) will have proven their belief in God's promise and enter the kingdom under God's blessing. Those who did not help the Jewish people will also have proven their true spiritual attitude and will be sent to the lake of fire for eternity.

THE MILLENIUM KINGDOM[120]

After the judgments are complete, there are several things that Jesus must do to make everything right so his kingdom may begin. One of these is a series of resurrections of believers who had died throughout the ages. Since God had promised the kingdom to the Old Testament saints, they must be resurrected so they can enter and enjoy the kingdom (Daniel 12:1-3). Those who had come to believe in Jesus and then died during the tribulation judgments will also be resurrected to enter the kingdom (Revelation 20:4-6). Since the church will return with Jesus at his second coming, all saints throughout history will be united for the first time and enter the kingdom together.

The Bible (especially in the Old Testament prophets) provides more details about the kingdom than any other single future event because this was the hope and anticipation of God's people for so long. It will be characterized by peace and righteousness, including how humans and animals will relate with each other again (Isaiah 11:1-9). Jesus will rule as king from a newly-rebuilt Jerusalem and temple, exhibiting all of God's wisdom in his decisions (Ezekiel 40-48; Psalm 2). Israel will be the center of God's attention, and the Jewish people will finally be respected and loved rather than hated, and the true God will be worshiped by all peoples (Zechariah 8:22-23). Satan

---

[120] The term millennium comes from the Latin words, *mille* ("thousand") and *annum* ("years"); the millennium as a term for Jesus' kingdom is the one thousand years in Revelation 20.

and his demons will be put away, unable to deceive humans, proving that any sins committed will come purely out of a human's sinful heart. According to Revelation 20:1-3, God will have Satan locked up for the one thousand years of the kingdom. This will not be his final judgment. At the end of the kingdom, God will release him for one last revolt before he is confined to the lake of fire forever (Revelation 20:7-10). Even under the utopian conditions of Jesus' kingdom, many people will want to rebel and will follow Satan as soon as they have the opportunity.

GREAT WHITE THRONE

Upon Satan's release at the end of the one thousand years and his final rebellion against Jesus, he will be judged and sent to the lake of fire forever, where the antichrist and false prophet are still in torment after one thousand years (Revelation 20:7-10).

Since all believers from all time were resurrected before the kingdom, only unbelievers will still be dead. After Satan's final defeat, all unbelievers from all time will stand before God for their final judgment.

> Then I saw a great white throne and him who was seated on it. From his presence earth and sky fled away, and no place was found for them. And I saw the dead, great and small, standing before the throne, and books were opened. Then another book was opened, which is the book of life. And the dead were judged by what was written in the books, according to what they had done. And the sea gave up the dead who were in it, death and Hades gave up the dead who were in them, and they were judged, each one of them, according to what they had done. Then

death and Hades were thrown into the lake of fire. This is the second death, the lake of fire. And if anyone's name was not found written in the book of life, he was thrown into the lake of fire (Revelation 20:11-15).

They will be judged on two counts: their works and their faith. Their lack of faith in Jesus will determine their final destiny to be the lake of fire forever, along with Satan. Much like a believer's good works will count toward eternal rewards, it seems an unbeliever's bad works will count toward eternal punishment. At this point, all people from the beginning of time will have been resurrected and judged, ready to begin the eternal state.

ETERNITY

The eternal state is what God had intended from the very beginning, the perfect environment—physical and relational—for God and people. Because sin has thoroughly corrupted the present creation, God will destroy heaven and earth, "making all things new" (2 Peter 3:10-13; Revelation 21:1). One of the most famous and anticipated Bible promises will finally occur at this time: "He will wipe away every tear from their eyes, and death shall be no more, neither shall there be mourning, nor crying, nor pain anymore, for the former things have passed away" (Revelation 21:4).

Revelation 21-22 gives a small picture of what eternity will be like. The earth will be full of nations representing their languages, customs, and cultures. The church will be reigning with Jesus, our responsibilities certainly part of the rewards based on our current faithfulness. "No longer will there be anything accursed, but the throne of God and of the Lamb will be in it, and his servants will worship him. They will see his face, and his name will be on their foreheads" (Revelation 22:3-4). The sun, moon, and night will be banished as God's eternal and infinite light radiates through a brand-new creation.

SUMMARY

The study of the end times is far more than arguing over unimportant details as many would have us think. If God decided to give us so much detail about the future, should we not make the effort to understand it, rather than setting it aside as unimportant? Believers are encouraged to be "looking for the blessed hope and the appearing of the glory of our great God and Savior, Christ Jesus" (Titus 2:13, NASB). Peter asks us to consider "what sort of people ought you to be in lives of holiness and godliness, waiting for and hastening the coming of the day of God" (2 Peter 3:11-12). We are to believe so much in the rapture of the church that we can encourage one another with that truth (1 Thessalonians 4:18; 5:11).

Finally, the weight of the knowledge of these coming events should cause us to prepare ourselves to share the gospel with all those who are willing to listen. It should not escape our notice that some of the final words of the Revelation—and the Bible itself—are a call for all people to come to Jesus.

> I, Jesus, have sent my angel to testify to you about these things for the churches. I am the root and the descendant of David, the bright morning star! And the Spirit and the bride say, "Come!" And let the one who hears say: "Come!" And let the one who is thirsty come; let the one who wants it take the water of life free of charge (Revelation 22:16-17, NET).

STUDY QUESTIONS

1. Has this chapter encouraged you to study the end times further? Why or why not?

2. After reading this chapter, how would you answer the three questions at the beginning?

   a. What happens to those who never believe in Jesus?

   b. What happens to those who believe in Jesus but never grow spiritually?

   c. What happens to those who believe in Jesus and make the effort to mature?

3. What is the most important truth, principle, or practice you learned from this chapter? What do you plan to do with it?

EPILOGUE

A FINAL THOUGHT

God's ultimate purpose in everything is to bring glory to himself. This is the reason he acts (and sometimes chooses not to act), and it is also the purpose for which he wants us to live.

> For my own sake, for my own sake, I do it, for how should my name be profaned? My glory I will not give to another (Isaiah 48:11).

> So, whether you eat or drink, or whatever you do, do all to the glory of God (1 Corinthians 10:31).

With that understanding, it is interesting to note the primary goal which He is working to accomplish. Many Bible students say that God's ultimate goal is to save us. Others point to the kingdom as the end of his plans. Scripture, however, provides a different picture, one that includes both salvation and the kingdom but is bigger than both of them.

What is God working toward? What has he always wanted? Where is he taking this whole thing? God has communicated his intention to be personally present among humans. This is one of the prominent narratives of the Bible. He will use salvation and the kingdom as ways to accomplish this, but the endgame is God and humans together, forever. Consider this survey through the Old and New Testaments that points out the many times God's presence is in focus, especially after sin ruined the initial attempt:

- Adam and Eve hid from God's presence after they sinned and then were banished from the garden and his presence (Genesis 3:8, 22-24).

- Cain was more afraid to be sent away from God's presence than the potential revenge his family might seek (Genesis 4:14, 16).

- Enoch "walked with God" so closely that God raptured him instead of allowing him to die (Genesis 5:21-24).

- Noah "walked with God" which set him apart from everyone else in his generation (Genesis 6:8-9).

- Abraham had such a close relationship with God that they ate meals together and Abraham felt comfortable enough to discuss and question God's plans and motives (Genesis 18).

- Moses lived and worked in God's presence on Mount Sinai and in the Tabernacle as he ruled over Israel (Exodus 33:7-11). He also prayed that God's presence would stay with Israel, stating that they had no hope without it (Exodus 33:12-15).

- God's presence was especially important to the people of Israel and was closely tied to their entire system of worship and, later, their monarchy.

  - On the Day of Atonement, they stood before the "presence of the Lord" (Leviticus 16).

  - The table holding the "bread of the presence" was in the tabernacle.

  - The sacrifices were made in God's presence and the feasts were celebrated in his presence.

  - Saul was established as king in God's presence (1 Samuel 11:15).

- It was when a new generation of Israelites grew up, having not experienced God's presence, that they rebelled and fell away leading to the time of the judges (Judges 2:7-10).

- The Psalms are full of David and the other writers longing to be in God's presence (Psalm 42:1-4).

- The prophecies about Messiah often include references to God's presence finally being with his people, including one that gives his title as "God with us" (Isaiah 7:14; 9:1-7).

- The Isaiah prophecy was revived seven hundred years later when Mary became pregnant with Jesus, the eternal Son of God, who would one day fulfill the Immanuel prophecy (Matthew 1:18-25).

- During his ministry, Jesus chose twelve men to be his apostles. This meant not only that they would do ministry with him but also "that they would be with him" (Mark 3:13-14).

- After Jesus' ascension, the apostles continued their ministry, opening themselves for persecution. At one point, Luke wrote that the Jewish religious leaders against them "were amazed and recognized these men had been with Jesus" (Acts 4:13).

- Finally, one day God's plan will be realized and "the residence of God is among human beings. He will live among them ... His servants will worship him, and they will see his face" (Revelation 21:3; 22:3-4).

This has always been God's plan—his glory on full display and celebrated through his personal dwelling with his highest created beings. For thousands of years he has been working and waiting to fulfill everything he promised and bring it to completion. Until then, the Holy Spirit lives in believers, helping us commit to Biblical discipleship and, ultimately, the rich, intimate knowledge of the Savior.

I have been crucified with Christ. It is no longer I who live, but Christ who lives in me. And the life I now live in the flesh I live by faith in the Son of God, who loved me and gave himself for me (Galatians 2:20).

His divine power has bestowed on us everything necessary for life and godliness through the rich knowledge of the one who called us by his own glory and excellence. ... if these things are really yours and are continually increasing, they will keep you from becoming ineffective and unproductive in your pursuit of knowing our Lord Jesus Christ more intimately (2 Peter 1:3, 8, NET).

Finally, as Peter puts it,

> Grow in the grace and knowledge of our Lord and Savior Jesus Christ. To him be the honor both now and on that eternal day (2 Peter 3:18).

SELECTED BIBLIOGRAPHY

Adams, Jay E. *Godliness Through Discipline*. Grand Rapids, MI: Baker Book House, 1972.

Alcorn, Randy. *Money, Possessions, and Eternity, Revised and Updated*. Carol Stream, IL: Tyndale House Publishers, Inc., 2003.

Benware, Paul N. *Understanding End Times Prophecy: A Comprehensive Approach*. Revised and Expanded. Chicago, IL: Moody Press, 2006.

Carson, D.A. *For the Love of God*, Volume 2. Wheaton, IL: Crossway Books, 1999. Kindle.

Chafer, Lewis Sperry. *He That is Spiritual*. Grand Rapids, MI: Zondervan, 1983.

Coleman, Robert E. *The Master Plan of Discipleship*. Grand Rapids, MI: Fleming H. Revell, 1998.

Friesen, Garry. *Decision Making and the Will of God*. Revised and Updated Edition. Colorado Springs, CO: Multnomah Books, 2004.

Fruchtenbaum, Arnold. *The Messianic Jewish Epistles*. San Antonio, TX: Ariel Ministries), 2004.

Geiger, Eric, Michael Kelley, Philip Nation. *Transformational Discipleship: How People Really Grow*. Nashville, TN: B&H Publishing Group, 2012.

Geisler, Norman. *Systematic Theology, Volume Four: Church, Last Things*. Minneapolis, MN: Bethany House Publishers, 2005.

Hitchcock, Mark. *Heavenly Rewards: Living with Eternity in Sight*. Eugene, OR: Harvest House Publishers, 2019.

Kitchen, Lucas. *Salvation and Discipleship: Is There a Difference?* Self-published, 2017.

Koehler, Ludwig et al., *The Hebrew and Aramaic Lexicon of the Old Testament*. Leiden, Netherlands: E.J. Brill, 1996.

Lane, Timothy S. and Paul David Tripp. *How People Change*. Greensboro, NC: New Growth Press, 2008.

Miles, Paul, ed. *What is Dispensationalism?* Wynnewood, OK: Grace Abroad Ministries, 2018.

Olson, C. Gordon. *Beyond Calvinism and Arminianism: An Inductive Mediate Theology of Salvation*. Third Edition Expanded, Revised, & Updated. Lynchburg, VA: Global Gospel Publishers, 2012.

Pentecost, J. Dwight. *Design for Discipleship: Discovering God's Blueprint for the Christian Life*. Grand Rapids, MI: Kregel Publications, 1996.

_____. *Things to Come: A Study in Biblical Eschatology.* Grand Rapids, MI: Zondervan Publishing House, 1958.

Putman, Jim. *Real-Life Discipleship: Building Churches that Make Disciples.* Colorado Springs, CO: NavPress, 2010.

Rainer, Thom S. *I Am a Church Member: Discovering the Attitude that Makes the Difference.* Nashville: B&H Publishing Group, 2013.

Ryrie, Charles C. *Balancing the Christian Life.* Chicago, IL: Moody Press, 1994.

_____. *Dispensationalism.* Chicago, IL: Moody Press, 2007.

Stanley, Andy. *The Principle of the Path.* Nashville: Thomas Nelson, 2008.